Profound and practical. Deep and detailed. If you've ever struggled to close the gap between good intentions and good actions, this book is for you. Pastor Craig masterfully challenges and equips us to predetermine to live in a way that maximizes productivity, blesses others, and glorifies God.

—**Louie Giglio,** pastor, Passion City Church; founder, Passion Conferences; author, *Don't Give the Enemy a Seat at Your Table*

We all get stuck. Pastor Craig throws us a rope to help us crawl out. God has given us the power to plan and imagine and choose and change; we just have to decide to partner with him and do it.

—**Jennie Allen,** *New York Times* bestselling author, *Find Your People* and *Get out of Your Head*; founder and visionary, IF:Gathering

Every day you have the chance to make your life count. In *Think Ahead,* my friend Pastor Craig teaches us how to create better habits and make great decisions. Let his wisdom, impact, and love for Christ help you be the best version of who God created you to be.

—**Tim Tebow,** former professional athlete; five-time *New York Times* bestselling author; founder, Tim Tebow Foundation

In a world where we are overwhelmed with competing options, Craig shows us how to make great decisions that are biblically based and scientifically proven. If you apply the principles outlined in *Think Ahead,* you will lead a flourishing and fruitful life. I loved this book from start to finish. Insightful. Honest. Hilarious. Practical. Life altering.

—**Christine Caine,** founder, A21 and Propel Women

I'm so excited about this new book by my good friend and pastor, Craig Groeschel. *Think Ahead* walks you through seven key decisions for a life that honors God. This isn't just another book, it's your guide to a meaningful life. If you're serious about moving in the direction of your purpose, this book is for you.

—**Steven Furtick,** lead pastor, Elevation Church; *New York Times* bestselling author, *Crash the Chatterbox*; *Greater*; *(Un)Qualified*; and *Do the New You*

Think Ahead is the right-now book for you if you are looking to refocus your thought life and improve your everyday habits. My wise friend Pastor Craig is the right teacher to lead us through a process of thinking ahead about the life we truly want to be living and how to get there. Get your copy today; it's truly a game changer.

—**Lysa TerKeurst,** *New York Times* bestselling author; president, Proverbs 31 Ministries

The practice of pre-deciding is like a GPS that will guide you to way better places than doing life without it. Craig has given us a real gift in a life-steering practice that will enable anyone to walk on much more solid ground. Highly recommend.

—**Dr. Henry Cloud**, psychologist; *New York Times* bestselling author

I've been blessed to call Craig Groeschel my friend for more than two decades, and he remains one of the most trusted and exceptional leaders I know. In *Think Ahead*, Craig reveals the secret to making great decisions by aligning our choices and behaviors with our core beliefs. Bringing the power of the gospel to the latest research on how to create healthier habits, Craig challenges us to apply God's timeless truth to every area of our lives. As practical as it is profound, *Think Ahead* will change your life.

—**Chris Hodges**, senior pastor, Church of the Highlands;
author, *Out of the Cave* and *Pray First*

In business and in life, hard decisions are going to come at you. In *Think Ahead*, Pastor Craig shows us proof that the quality of our decisions is exponentially increased by knowing what we believe and why we believe it. By pre-deciding, we only have to walk through the victory or pain of the result, but not the pain of indecision. Another must-read from my friend Craig Groeschel.

—**Dave Ramsey**, bestselling author

Most people think success is about working hard, getting a little lucky, or being given a leg up. All of this is true, of course, but none of those reasons will guarantee success. The truth is, over time, the only behavior that ensures success is good decision-making. Each of us is only about a thousand good decisions away from a life we dream about. So the key is to learn to make great decisions and then make them every day. In *Think Ahead*, Craig Groeschel, who has lived this message for decades, teaches us how to make decisions that will shape our lives for the better.

—**Donald Miller**, author, *Building a StoryBrand*

When I was young, I thought you had to make a choice in life: success or peace. You could be successful, stewarding your talents with excellence, or you could be peaceful; it was an either-or situation. But Craig Groeschel showed me how wrong I was. I've been friends with him for more than ten years, and it's hard to think of someone who does a better job balancing peace and performance. How does he do it? Well, fortunately for us, he writes books in which he shares his secrets. At some point, maybe I'll retire the sentence, "This is Craig's best book!" because I feel like I say it every time he releases a new one, but it's true. This is Craig's best book!

—**Jon Acuff**, *New York Times* bestselling author, *All It Takes Is a Goal*

It can be so frustrating to be stuck at point A and want to get to point B but just don't know how. I'm so grateful to Craig Groeschel for showing us the way to get unstuck from the habits that hold us back so we can get to where God wants us to be.

—**Bob Goff,** *New York Times* bestselling author, *Love Does*; *Everybody, Always*; *Dream Big*; and *Undistracted*

It's one thing to recognize that you consistently make poor choices. It's another thing to be motivated enough to change your decision-making patterns. In *Think Ahead*, Craig gives you an incredibly helpful blueprint filled with biblical truth, research, and his own experience. It's everything you need to motivate you to take that first step on a journey of living God's plans for your life.

—**John C. Maxwell,** bestselling leadership author; mentor; coach

When was the last time you reflected on the quality of your daily actions and how you choose to live? *Think Ahead* is an insightful masterpiece of decision-making tools that just changed my life.

—**Cynt Marshall,** CEO, Dallas Mavericks; president and CEO, Marshalling Resources Consulting

Pastor Craig has always been someone I've looked up to when it comes to real-life application and biblical principles. His new book, *Think Ahead*, continues to push me and challenge me, and I'm so thankful he wrote it!

—**Rachel Cruze,** *New York Times* bestselling author; personal finance expert

As I've gotten to know Pastor Craig Groeschel, I'm convinced he's the best person of our day to instruct us on life and leadership. *Think Ahead* is a brilliant work of his best practices simplified into seven decisions. I can't wait to read it again with my small group. You are going to enjoy learning from the life-changing practices in the pages ahead.

—**Jonathan Pokluda,** lead pastor, Harris Creek Baptist Church; bestselling author; host, *Becoming Something* podcast

If you've ever felt like you're waiting on God's plans to unfold and are not sure why nothing seems to be happening, then let Craig Groeschel's *Think Ahead* be your playbook. Craig challenges all of us to make seven critical pre-decisions that change everything. It's practical, challenging, and immensely convicting. I'll be coming back to this book again and again.

—**Carey Nieuwhof,** bestselling author, *At Your Best*; podcaster; founder, The Art of Leadership Academy

An incredible read and step-by-step guide on how to make life's most important decisions.

—**Stephanie Chung,** aviation executive; international speaker; board member

There is no one better to share wisdom and insight on the power of pre-deciding than Craig. His life shouts "think ahead." And in this book, he teaches us the power of pre-deciding thoughts so we can accomplish and steward all God wants to do in and through us. Using personal experience, biblical truths, and scientific research, Craig helps us learn how to break through the cycle of making bad decisions and gives us tools to make great decisions that will have a lasting impact on our future and the world around us.

—**Earl McClellan,** senior pastor, Shoreline City Church

Craig has done it again! Such practical and useful wisdom on every page. Living a God-honoring life is attainable for everyone who calls themselves a Christian.

—**Jentezen Franklin,** senior pastor, Free Chapel;
author, *New York Times* bestselling *Fasting*

Lots of people can give advice, but not everyone can give practical, biblical advice the way Pastor Craig does. This guy just simply gets it done in a God-honoring way that helps other people be in the position to do the same.

—**Michael Jr.,** comedian; author; thought leader

In the modern, technological, and fast-paced world we live in, we end up deciding on things and situations that do not always reflect what we would like to have chosen. In this book, Pastor Craig brings biblical and scientific foundations that help us think and decide in line with our real identity as a child of God.

—**Kaká (Richardo Leite),** Brazilian soccer player
(retired); FIFA World Player of the Year 2007

There is a Chinese proverb that says, "The best time to plant a tree is ten years ago, but the second best time is right now." In *Think Ahead*, my friend Craig Groeschel gives you what you wish you had put into motion in your life a decade ago—practical, actionable steps toward a more intentional, abundant life. There will definitely be "aha" moments where you will kick yourself for not knowing or doing these things sooner, but ten years from now, you will be glad you got your hands on this book right now.

—**Levi Lusko,** author, *Marvel at the Moon: 90 Devotions:
You're Never Alone in God's Majestic Universe*

THINK
AHEAD

Also by Craig Groeschel

Altar Ego: Becoming Who God Says You Are

Chazown: Discover and Pursue God's Purpose for Your Life

The Christian Atheist: Believing in God but Living As If He Doesn't Exist

Daily Power: 365 Days of Fuel for Your Soul

Dangerous Prayers: Because Following Jesus Was Never Meant to Be Safe

Dare to Drop the Pose (previously titled *Confessions of a Pastor*)

Divine Direction: Seven Decisions That Will Change Your Life

Fight: Winning the Battles That Matter Most

From This Day Forward: Five Commitments to Fail-Proof Your Marriage (with Amy Groeschel)

Hope in the Dark: Believing God Is Good When Life Is Not

Lead Like It Matters: Seven Leadership Principles for a Church That Lasts (previously titled *It: How Churches and Leaders Can Get It and Keep It*)

Liking Jesus: Intimacy and Contentment in a Selfie-Centered World (previously titled *#Struggles*)

Love, Sex, and Happily Ever After (previously titled *Going All the Way*)

The Power to Change: Mastering the Habits That Matter Most

Soul Detox: Clean Living in a Contaminated World

Weird: Because Normal Isn't Working

What Is God Really Like? (general editor)

Winning the War in Your Mind: Change Your Thinking, Change Your Life

THINK AHEAD

7 DECISIONS YOU CAN MAKE TODAY FOR THE GOD-HONORING LIFE YOU WANT TOMORROW

CRAIG GROESCHEL

NEW YORK TIMES BESTSELLING AUTHOR

ZONDERVAN
BOOKS

ZONDERVAN BOOKS

Think Ahead
Copyright © 2024 by Craig Groeschel

Published in Grand Rapids, Michigan, by Zondervan. Zondervan is a registered trademark of The Zondervan Corporation, L.L.C., a wholly owned subsidiary of HarperCollins Christian Publishing, Inc.

Requests for information should be addressed to customercare@harpercollins.com.

Zondervan titles may be purchased in bulk for educational, business, fundraising, or sales promotional use. For information, please email SpecialMarkets@Zondervan.com.

ISBN 978-0-310-36853-3 (international trade paper edition)
ISBN 978-0-310-36658-4 (audio)

Library of Congress Cataloging-in-Publication Data

Names: Groeschel, Craig, author.
Title: Think ahead : 7 decisions you can make today for the God-honoring life you want tomorrow / Craig Groeschel.
Description: Grand Rapids : Zondervan, 2024.
Identifiers: LCCN 2023029696 (print) | LCCN 2023029697 (ebook) | ISBN 9780310366560 (hardcover) | ISBN 9780310366577 (ebook)
Subjects: LCSH: Decision-making—Religious aspects—Christianity. | Problem solving—Religious aspects—Christianity. | Christian life. | BISAC: EDUCATION / Decision-Making & Problem Solving | SELF-HELP / Personal Growth / Success
Classification: LCC BV4599.5.P75 G76 2024 (print) | LCC BV4599.5.P75 (ebook) | DDC 248.4—dc23/eng/20230927
LC record available at https://lccn.loc.gov/2023029696
LC ebook record available at https://lccn.loc.gov/2023029697

Craig Groeschel is represented by Thomas J. Winters of Winters & King, Inc., Tulsa, Oklahoma.

Cover design: James W. Hall IV
Cover illustrations: © Dasha Yurk / © Sergii / Adobe Stock
Interior design: Denise Froehlich

Printed in the United States of America

23 24 25 26 27 LBC 5 4 3 2 1

Contents

Introduction: The Power of Pre-Deciding 1

Part 1: I Will Be Ready

1.1 The Man in the Mirror 17
1.2 I'm Ready 22
1.3 Move the Line 26
1.4 Magnify the Cost 32
1.5 Plan Your Escape 36
1.6 Your Weak Spot 40

Part 2: I Will Be Devoted

2.1 What Lies Beneath 47
2.2 What a Devoted Life Looks (and Doesn't Look) Like 52
2.3 The (Shocking) Power of Connection 57
2.4 Distracted from Devotion...................................... 62
2.5 Your Rule and a Game Plan 66

Part 3: I Will Be Faithful

3.1 One Word 79
3.2 Every Interaction Is an Opportunity to Add Value 82
3.3 Every Resource Is an Opportunity to Multiply 88
3.4 Every Prompting Is an Opportunity to Obey God 93
3.5 Free to Risk...97
3.6 Vastly Underestimating 102

Part 4: I Will Be an Influencer

4.1   Are You an Influencer?.. 109

4.2   I Will Influence with My Prayers........................... 112

4.3   I Will Influence with My Example 119

4.4   I Will Influence with My Words............................ 127

4.5   The Long Game 131

Part 5: I Will Be Generous

5.1   How to Be More Blessed 137

5.2   Stop Holding Back.. 143

5.3   Generous People Plan to Be Generous..................... 146

5.4   Generous People Round Up.................................. 155

5.5   Standing Firm in Generosity 159

Part 6: I Will Be Consistent

6.1   Inconsistent Anonymous 167

6.2   The Power of Consistency 171

6.3   Start with Why...176

6.4   Plan to Fail 181

6.5   Fall in Love with the Process 186

6.6   But I Can't 189

Part 7: I Will Be a Finisher

7.1   Voting on Your Future 197

7.2   True Grit... 202

7.3   Quitting.. 206

7.4   Take Another Step 211

Conclusion: Pre-Choose This Day 219

Acknowledgments.. 227

Appendix: Takeaways and Scriptures............................... 229

Notes 263

Introduction

The Power of Pre-Deciding

35,000.

Seven.

35,000 is the number shaping your life.

Seven is the number that will allow you to take back your life.

Before I explain these numbers, I want to begin with a story to give you an example of how I have struggled with decision-making.

Spider-Man, a Typewriter, and a Pay Phone

It was the early '90s and I was in my early twenties. I was newly married and a full-time pastor at First United Methodist Church in Oklahoma City. I was also a full-time seminary student.

Go back and read that last paragraph again. Look for the first sign that I have issues. Newly married and a full-time pastor? Okay. Newly married and a full-time seminary student? Sure. But newly married and a full-time pastor and a full-time seminary student? I was young, had a calling from God, and was ready to take on the world, so of course I thought I was bulletproof.

In that era, girls wore leg warmers, shoulder pads, and big hoop earrings. Guys wore acid-washed jeans, Jams shorts, and the ever-coveted Members Only jackets. Back when Bon Jovi was livin' on a prayer. And when people did not yet own personal computers. Well, maybe a few did, but I certainly didn't. So I wrote my papers for seminary on a typewriter. For those under forty, go ahead and take a moment to google "typewriter."

One night I stayed really late at the church typing a fifteen-page paper for a class. The next morning, when I got up early for the ninety-minute drive to seminary, I realized I'd left my paper in my office. *Ugh.* Since I had typed the paper there, the copy sitting on my desk was the only one in the world. I had to go back and get it.

So at 6:00 a.m. I drove to the church. What I didn't realize was that our key cards were programmed not to open the doors until 8:00 a.m. I tried, but the door wouldn't unlock, and I had to get that paper.

That's when I made the first in a series of bad decisions.

My office was on the third floor of our majestic church building. Because it was up so high, I always left my window unlocked, knowing no one would be dumb enough to risk the dangerous climb to break in. No one except me. Since the window was my only option, I thought, *I could just climb up the wall to my window.*

Over the years, I have since discovered a lot about myself—abilities I possess and others I lack. But at that moment I did not yet know whether I might be Spider-Man. It was time to find out.

I was actually able to climb the wall! (The exclamation point is because that's the only positive thing I get to say about myself in this entire story.) After carefully scaling the wall and arriving at my window, I precariously perched in my penny loafers on the small ledge. With my left hand, I held on to a brick in the building with my fingertips. I cautiously reached down with my right and tried to lift the window. It wouldn't budge. Someone had locked it!

At that moment I realized I was in big trouble. I couldn't turn around or go back down. I was stuck there. Talk about livin' on a prayer! It was now 6:20 a.m. This was before everyone had cell phones, so I had no way of calling anyone. What did I do? I just stayed there. Well, more like hung on there, with the toes of my loafers on the ledge and my fingers in the brick crevices. I started singing to myself, *Oh, we've got to hold on, ready or not. You live for the fight when it's all that you've got. Whoa oh, we're halfway there. Whoa oh, livin' on a prayer.*

About thirty minutes later I saw a guy walking down the street. I started shouting. "Hey! Help! Up here! No, up here! It's me, the guy in the pleated khaki pants and Members Only jacket! The guy three stories above you. Hey!" Finally, this apparently directionally or visually impaired stranger saw me and yelled up that he would get help. How? He had to find a pay phone. For those under thirty, take a moment to google "pay phone."

Evidently he found one, because soon the fire department showed up to get Pastor Craig down off the wall from the third story of the historic church building.

Now, why do I tell you all that?

To let you know that I can be a poor decision-maker.

I hate to break it to you, but chances are you can be a poor decision-maker too. No offense, but it turns out we can all be pretty bad at making decisions.

And that's a big deal, because this is true for any of us:

The quality of our decisions determines the quality of our lives.

We'll get to the importance of our decisions in a moment, but now that I've said you and I can be poor decision-makers, I think I owe it to you to explain why we all make poor decisions.

The Three Enemies of Excellent Decisions

You want to make great decisions. So do I.

You may even want to believe that the majority of the time you do make great decisions. So do I.

But we don't. We can all admit that, right? Just look at the evidence:

- We eat more than we should.
- We buy things we can't afford.
- We waste time.
- We procrastinate.
- We say things we regret.
- We do things we don't want to do.
- We hurt the people we love most.
- We don't do things we want to do.
- We don't eat healthy food, exercise, read our Bibles, or save for the future.

- We don't pray enough, say "I love you" enough, or slow down enough.

We can be really bad at decision-making.

Even the apostle Paul admitted his frustrating battle with decisions. He was bluntly honest in Romans 7:19: "I want to do what is good, but I don't. I don't want to do what is wrong, but I do it anyway" (NLT). Proof that everyone struggles with this issue.

Speaking of bad decisions, did you hear about the guy who had a cockroach living in his ear for three days but thought it was just water, so he kept blow-drying his ear?[1] Hopefully we at least have an edge on that dude.

So if we want to make great decisions, what's stopping us?

The technical answer is *lots*.

So many things.

But I will highlight three.

Enemy of Excellent Decisions 1: We're Overwhelmed

I started this introduction with the number 35,000. Here's where it comes into play. Experts estimate that we make 35,000 decisions a day.[2] A day! Wow. That can only mean that you and I are making decisions all day, every day, like these:

- whether to hit snooze
- whether to take time to pray
- what to wear
- what to eat
- whether to exercise
- whether to post on social media, what to post, and what posts to like
- to dodge or not to dodge a coworker
- when to check email and how to respond to every email
- what to do tonight and what to do this weekend

While 35,000 decisions sounds unbelievable at first, once we start to think about all of the subconscious and split-second calls like these that we make, that huge number makes sense. One thing is for certain: the decisions never stop coming.

That's why it can be so overwhelming. We make so many choices that our decision-making muscle becomes tired. Cognitive scientists call it "decision fatigue." They've discovered this:

> As the volume of decisions increases,
> the quality of decisions decreases.

One group of experts offered this explanation: "Individuals experiencing decision fatigue demonstrate an impaired ability to make trade-offs, prefer a passive role in the decision-making process, and often make choices that seem impulsive or irrational."[3]

That explains why you can make difficult and wise decisions all day at work and then at night binge-eat and waste several hours staring at a screen. It's because you got tired of making good decisions. Or perhaps you've been making a series of wise financial choices because you want to save money, but then, out of nowhere, you make an irrational purchase you later regret. You wonder, *How could I be so stupid? Why did I do that?*

The answer is decision fatigue.

The first enemy of excellent decision-making is that we're bombarded with too many decisions.

In your decision-making, are you overwhelmed? Fatigued?

Enemy of Excellent Decisions 2: We're Afraid

We don't worry about whether to eat oatmeal or yogurt for breakfast, but when it comes to bigger decisions, we are often afraid of making the wrong choice. *Should I buy this car? Should I take this job offer? Should I move?*

Ever hear of analysis paralysis? We look at all of the options and then freeze up out of fear that we'll make the wrong decision.

This problem is exacerbated for Christians because we have the added challenge of trying to discern God's will. So the always difficult question of what's the right thing to do is further complicated by the fear that we might miss out on God's plan. Like, *What if I miss out on the perfect situation he has for me? What if I settle? Or worse, what if I mess up and it takes years to get my life back on track?*

All of this can lead us to make a bad choice. But sometimes, because we're not sure, we just don't make a decision at all. That feels safer, but we have to remember:

Indecision is a decision and often the enemy of progress.

So when making decisions, how often are you afraid? How often is your decision not to decide?

Enemy of Excellent Decisions 3: We're Emotional

In their book *Decisive*, Chip Heath and Dan Heath show through their extensive research that we are biologically hardwired to act foolishly and behave irrationally.[4] They explain that our emotions may be the preeminent enemy of excellent decisions. We let emotion overrule logic.

You've experienced this. You don't want to yell at your children. But then your kid does something dumb. Logic says, *Be patient.* But emotion says, *Yell as loudly as you can.* And emotion overrules logic.

Or there's a sin you are determined to avoid. But then temptation comes knocking. Logic says, *Doing that is not healthy and dishonors God.* But emotion says, *Let's party!* Emotion overrules logic.

To make great decisions we need to think ahead, to ask, *What are the consequences of this choice? What path does this decision put me on?* But emotions typically give us a myopic focus on the here and now.

What's interesting is that we often spend way too much time analyzing unimportant decisions (*Which Netflix show should I binge-watch next?*) but make important decisions (*Should I watch porn?*) on an emotional whim. An embarrassing personal example: I once spent hours researching a purchase on Amazon. The big decision? Whether to buy the seven-dollar version with the 5-star rating or the six-dollar version with the 4.5-star rating. I started reading through all 4,328 reviews to determine the wise choice. But when it comes to critical decisions, I often let my emotions take over and I just react in the moment. (Like deciding to scale a three-story building.)

Obviously, forces are working against our making wise choices.

So on any given day, how many decisions do you make based on your emotions?

Let's stop and review. Because the quality of our decisions determines the quality of our lives, we must understand the three enemies of excellent choices:

1. Overwhelm
2. Fear
3. Emotion

The Sum of Your Life

It's safe to say that life is the sum of the decisions we make. Why? Because a successful life is based not on a few big decisions made at a few big moments but on thousands of normal decisions made at thousands of normal moments.

As James Clear says, "Every decision you make is a vote toward who you will become." That's why we need to think ahead. That's why we *have* to think ahead. Each seemingly inconsequential decision has such value because our decisions are rarely isolated. Have you noticed how good decisions tend to compound in the right direction and bad decisions tend to compound in the wrong direction?

I bet you've made a bad decision thinking it was only a one-time thing, then later realized it put you on a slippery path. It felt like that choice gave you permission to keep making the same choice or similarly bad ones. Somehow your bad decision multiplied.

You've also made good decisions that seemed isolated, but weren't at all. Your choice seemed normal, but it was actually enormous. You made the right choice and somehow it had a compound effect. It's like this:

We make our decisions, and then our decisions make us.

The decisions you make today determine the stories you tell tomorrow.

C. S. Lewis, a brilliant Christian thinker and author, wrote about this in his book *Mere Christianity*: "Good and evil both increase at compound interest. That is why the little decisions you and I make every day are of such infinite importance. The smallest good act today is the capture of a strategic point from which, a few months later, you may be able to go on to victories you never dreamed of. An apparently trivial indulgence in lust or anger today is the loss of a ridge or railway line or bridgehead from which the enemy may launch an attack otherwise impossible."[5]

> Your decisions determine your direction,
> and your direction determines your destiny.

So if your life is moving in the direction of your decisions, do you like the direction your decisions are taking you?

Do you feel good about who you are and where you are in life? Do you believe God is pleased with your direction?

If not, it's time to take back your life.

How?

Through the power of pre-decision.

The Power of Pre-Decision

You will decide *now* what you will do *later*.

You will *decide* now what you will *do* later.

That might sound simplistic, but it is a profound spiritual tool that will help you live in a forward-looking, people-loving, God-glorifying way that leads you to become who you want to become and live the life you want to live.

Decide now what you will do later.

When you're in the moment, the three enemies we just talked about wreak havoc on your ability to make quality decisions, so why wait until you are in the moment to decide?

> Ask God to help you decide now what you will do later.

With his help, what you do now can be different from what you did before on your own. We get stuck thinking, *I've always been this way, always done these things. It is what it is, I am what I am.* But God says, "Forget the former things; do not dwell on the past. See, I am doing a new thing!" (Isa. 43:18–19). We partner with God in the new thing he wants to do in our lives by making new decisions. We make these decisions with God and submit them to him. And what does God do? "Commit to the LORD whatever you do, and he will establish your plans" (Prov. 16:3).

Decide now what you will do later.

Look at the heroes of our faith throughout the Bible.

In Genesis 22, God told Abraham to sacrifice his son Isaac. Um, no one is going to decide to do that in the moment. But in the past Abraham had pre-decided, *My God is always trustworthy, so whatever he asks me to do, I will obey and honor him.* (Thankfully, God let good ol' Abe off the hook.)

In Ruth chapter one, we find Ruth and her sister Orpah with their mother-in-law, Naomi. Times are tough and getting worse. Naomi is headed back to her hometown, where her prospects are no better. Naomi tells the girls to stay and make new, better lives for themselves. It is the choice that gives them the best chances, so Orpah agrees to leave. But Ruth had pre-decided to make Naomi her ride-or-die: *Where you go, I will go. Where you stay, I will stay. Your God will be my God.*

Ruth had pre-decided her commitment to Naomi.

Then there's Daniel. He and his friends were essentially taken hostage and forced to live in a foreign land. Constant attempts were made to brainwash them into thinking like their captors and eating the food they ate. Yet Daniel believed eating the king's food would dishonor God. We read in Daniel 1:8, "But Daniel resolved . . ." We could say, "Daniel pre-decided." It says, "But Daniel resolved not to defile himself with the royal food and wine, and he asked the chief official for permission not to defile himself this way."

Daniel didn't wait to get to the dining room, where he might have been tempted to go against his values by the perfectly seared tomahawk ribeye and the molten-chocolate lava cake. No, he pre-decided, *My values will be determined by God, not others. I will honor my God with my choices.*

Daniel pre-decided his commitment to God.

When we decide now what we will do later, with God's help, we will determine our course of action before the moment of decision. It will look like this:

> When faced with [situation], I have pre-decided to [action].

For instance: "When I begin to worry, I will read 1 Peter 5:7, pray, and give the burden to God."

Or "When I'm tempted to make an impulse purchase of more than fifty dollars, I will wait at least three days before I decide whether to buy it."

Or "When I have written an angry email, I will sleep on it before deciding to hit send."

If you were to start applying everything we have discussed so far in making pre-decisions, how might that positively affect your life? Here are three immediate benefits:

1. Pre-Deciding Reduces the Number of Decisions to Make

Pre-deciding combats feeling overwhelmed by all of our choices, which can lead to decision fatigue. Steve Jobs famously wore the same outfit every day. Did he just really love his black turtleneck, Levi's 501s, and New Balance sneakers? No. But he knew that not having to choose his clothes every day freed up energy for more important decisions.

Billionaire hedge-fund manager Ray Dalio wrote a book about pre-deciding. In his book *Principles: Life and Work,* Dalio writes, "Without principles, we would be forced to react to all the things life throws at us individually, as if we were experiencing each of them for the first time." He goes on to say: "Using principles is a way of both simplifying and improving your decision making. . . . [This] will allow you to massively reduce the number of decisions you have to make (I estimate by a factor of something like 100,000) and will lead you to make much better ones."[6]

2. Pre-Deciding Reduces the Fear of Deciding Wrong

We often make poor choices because we are driven or stopped by fear. We fear with good reason: because we know our record and how much we have fighting against us in the moment of decision.

But pre-deciding reduces our fear. Why? Because we base our decisions on our values. We discover, in advance, what is important to God and decide what is important to us, and we commit to make decisions that honor those values. In the pages to come, I hope to help you find clarity on what is important to you. We're going to discover that when our values are clear, our decisions are easier.

3. Pre-Deciding Prevents Emotion from Taking Over

We want to live wise, God-honoring lives, but in the moment, our emotions often take over and hijack our integrity. That's why we need to decide before the moment. That way, our emotions don't get a vote.

It has been proven that this concept is the key to doing what you want to do. Peter Gollwitzer, a psychology professor at NYU, reviewed ninety-four studies that analyzed the effectiveness of pre-deciding by people who actually implement their best intentions. He concluded that having goals is no guarantee of success, because it doesn't account for the barriers that will arise along the way. So what did ensure success? Pre-deciding what to do when faced with such barriers.[7]

In another study, 368 people in orthopedic rehabilitation were split into two groups. One group set goals. The other set goals and also pre-decided what they would do to achieve them. Only those in the second group achieved their goals.[8]

When we pre-decide, we let logic overrule emotion.

Seven

You're probably wondering, "What should I pre-decide? It feels like the options are endless. I mean, do I need to wear the same outfit every day like Steve Jobs? If so, does it have to be as drab?"

At the beginning of this introduction, I gave you two numbers: 35,000 and seven. I said, "35,000 is the number shaping your life. Seven is the number that will allow you to take back your life."

Now that I've explained the 35,000 in detail, it's time for the seven.

I want to offer seven life-defining pre-decisions we all need to make. You may choose to add others, but I think you will see why these are so foundational as we journey together in the pages to come.

To get started, I want to be a little more honest with you than is comfortable for me. While I am a follower of Jesus, and I am a pastor, I have noticed some negative qualities in me.

- *I am unprepared.* I am often unprepared spiritually. Satan is the enemy of my soul. He attacks me at every opportunity. In those moments, I sometimes have my guard down. I love God with all my heart and truly want to follow Jesus, but actually doing that happens moment by moment, and I find that, in too many moments, my devotion falls short.

- *I am selfish.* I don't want to be, but I am. Because I am selfish, it's easier for me to want to get than to give. I am committed to the mission God has given us because I am convinced everyone needs Jesus. But I'm afraid that rather than being compelled to share the good news of God's love, too often I can be selfish with it.

- *I am inconsistent.* I find myself starting off in the right direction, but it's too easy for me to change course and end up doing the wrong thing. When things get tough, I want to give up and quit. Just walking away often feels like the best option.

Now that my confession is over, can I ask, Do you resonate with any of my issues? I described me, but did I also describe you?

If so, I'm sure, like me, that is not who you want to be or how you want to live.

Are you ready to think ahead and take your life back?

We can, through seven life-defining pre-decisions:

1. I will be ready.
2. I will be devoted.
3. I will be faithful.
4. I will be an influencer.
5. I will be generous.
6. I will be consistent.
7. I will be a finisher.

Are you ready to choose who you will become?

To live the life you want to live?

To be satisfied, to be successful, and to honor God?

Let's do this!

Let's pre-decide.

INTRODUCTION EXERCISES

1. Rate your day-to-day decision-making ability on a scale from 1 to 10 (low to high). Explain your answer.
2. How would your rating change as you move through the major areas of your life, such as family, work, friends, and spiritual life? Explain.
3. Are you fearful about making a decision? What area of your life tends to bring fear when you have to decide?
4. Is there an ongoing situation that causes decision fatigue? If so, what are some factors that contribute? (For example, volume, expectations, burden of importance.)
5. Are you feeling overwhelmed about making a decision? What area of your life tends to cause overwhelm when you have to decide?
6. Do you struggle with indecision or procrastination? Does it tend to be overall or just in certain situations? Be specific.
7. Are you feeling emotion about making a decision? What area of your life tends to cause emotion when you have to decide?
8. How often do you avoid important decisions by distracting yourself with unimportant ones? Does that tend to happen regularly in any area of your life?
9. Looking at your previous answers, can you detect any patterns where pre-deciding could benefit you? If so, write down your thoughts.
10. If you are a Christian, how does your relationship with God affect your decision-making? What are some benefits? Where do you struggle?

PART 1

I Will Be Ready

A prudent person foresees danger and takes precautions.
The simpleton goes blindly on and suffers the consequences.

—PROVERBS 27:12 NLT

The Man in the Mirror

I woke up, looked at myself in the mirror, and said, "I hate you."

I did. I hated what I saw because I had fallen again. I couldn't keep doing this. I needed a new plan to battle temptation.

Have you been there?

I'm going to guess you have.

I also know you didn't plan to be there.

You didn't plan to get addicted.

Or have your kids resent you.

You didn't hope to be someone with a disorder or an anger problem or a control issue or chronic unforgiveness.

You didn't want to be greedy or bitter.

I don't know anyone who had a five-year goal to bankrupt themselves financially or wreck their marriage.

No one plans on making a stupid in-the-moment decision, then hiding it, then lying about it, then losing trust with the people they love the most.

No one plans to mess up their lives.

The problem is they don't plan not to.

But they were not prepared when temptation knocked.

That's what happened to me the night before I despised my reflection in the mirror.

Temptation knocked.

And because I was not ready, I opened the door to the devil.

The Whispers

I've found that temptation whispers. Typically, it doesn't come blaring at you like a Metallica concert. Its vibe is more of an acoustic singer-songwriter playing in the back of a coffee shop. It's a subtle siren's call. See if you've heard any of these whispers:

- You've already sinned by being tempted, so you might as well.

Too many Christians have bought this lie, so to be super clear, it is not a sin to be tempted.

It *is* a sin to act on temptation.

But to be tempted is not sin, it is human.

Everyone is tempted.

Following Jesus doesn't guarantee the absence of temptation, it's a declaration of war against temptation.

Jesus himself, when he lived a human life on earth, was tempted. Matthew 4 details his three temptations in the desert, which came directly from Satan. Each time, Jesus refused and did not choose sin. That's why Hebrews 4 says he empathizes with our weakness, because he "has been tempted in every way, just as we are—yet he did not sin" (v. 15).

If you feel guilty because you were tempted—you noticed an attractive person jogging down the street, you considered lying to your boss about why you were fifteen minutes late to his Zoom call, you really wanted to eat your kid's Halloween candy—that is false guilt. You don't need to feel bad, because it's not a sin to be tempted.

And the whispers continue:

- Go ahead, you deserve it.
- God is holding back on you.
- No one has the right to tell you what you can do.
- It won't hurt if you do it just this once.
- No one is going to know.

Temptation whispers, and as we get lulled by it, we miss what it's doing. With a closer look, we'll see a consistent process:

1. *Temptation typically starts with a thought.* That thought may be triggered by something you see or someone's suggestion,

like "I've been working really hard lately. I deserve to do something fun."

2. *The next phase happens in your imagination.* You start to think about the leftover chocolate cake or your friend who can get you those pills or the video you know you shouldn't watch but kind of want to.

3. *Next comes justification.* You know you shouldn't, so you come up with reasons why you should. It's not that big a deal. No one's perfect. What's a little fun going to hurt?

4. *Then, finally, you make the choice.* Well, I guess I'll just eat a small piece (which turns into all of it) or take one pill or just glance at the video for a minute or two.

You sin.

And you don't want to sin.

But we have to understand that steps 1, 2, and 3 are all moments of temptation when we can still stop, turn away, say no, and make the right decision. Sin doesn't happen until step 4.

Sin Is Fun, Until It Isn't

It might not be what you hear from most pastors, but sin usually feels good. Right? It's fun. If you don't think sin is fun, then either

1. you are lying, or
2. you didn't do it right.

Sin is fun, until it's not. And it's usually not fun for long. A friend of mine says, "Sin thrills and then it kills. It fascinates, then it assassinates." (My friend is great at rhyming.)

Sin promises satisfaction, then robs us of what we want most. Why? Because every time we sin, we are missing out on God's best. Choosing to sin is choosing to live a less-than life. No one would ever choose a less-than life, but we do, because it's never mentioned in sin's sales pitch.

Because we love God, we don't want to sin. We know that sin breaks his heart. In the Bible we get the idea that sin is like committing adultery against God. We go behind his back, turn away from his love, and choose something else over him. Or we could say sin is choosing to love yourself even if it offends God. And sin does offend God. One more thing about sin: it separates us from God and leads to death.

James tells us, "Each person is tempted when they are dragged away by their own evil desire and enticed. Then, after desire has conceived, it gives birth to sin; and sin, when it is full-grown, gives birth to death" (James 1:14–15).

The analogy is a pregnancy: the seed is temptation that creates the conception of sin that leads to the birth of death. Death refers to separation. When we sin, we're separated from what God wants for us. We experience guilt and shame that rob us of the peace and joy we are meant to experience. When we sin, we're separated from God and lose intimacy with him.

Wow, that's a great reason to take temptation seriously.

Most people don't plan to sin. But they still do. Why? One reason is what's called the "either-or fallacy" (or "false dilemma" or "false dichotomy" fallacy), which is partly why we're such poor decision-makers. We often end up making wrong choices because we see only two options:

- Option A: Fight against temptation.
- Option B: Give in to temptation.

But with God there is another, better option many Jesus followers overlook:

- Option C: Pre-decide to avoid temptation.

With God's help, we're wise to make up our minds ahead of time to avoid temptation. We will choose to stay as far away as possible from what will hurt us and others and pre-decide:

I will be ready.

We can do that. I'm living proof. Let me tell you why I hated the me that looked back at me in the mirror and what happened next.

I became a Christ follower as a partying college frat boy. When I met Jesus and came to understand God's unconditional love, I had a grace explosion. I didn't want to sin anymore. I knew I had to quit getting drunk. And, by the power of Jesus, I stopped. I did not have another drink—until I went on a road trip.

When a few girls at the party said, "You look like Tom Cruise," my ego took off. I could hear the theme song from *Top Gun* and pictured myself playing beach volleyball with no shirt on. These girls were drinking beer. So I drank a beer. And another. And another. And another. And the next morning I woke up disgusted at myself. I painfully realized that I was not as strong as I'd thought and far more vulnerable than I'd imagined.

I didn't plan to get totally wasted and humiliate myself.

But I also didn't plan not to.

That was the last time I was drunk.

Not because I got stronger, but because I got ready.

I'm Ready

I must admit, I was not ready.

I've thought through so many scenarios. I'm prepared if a burglar breaks into my house. (My nunchucks are always within reach beside the bed. You don't want to mess with me!) I am ready for salesmen who walk up and knock on my door. (Hiding always works.) And I know what to do when I walk up on Girl Scouts selling cookies. (Turn and run as fast and as far as I can.)

I am ready for all those scenarios.

I was not ready for the bobcat.

Innocently walking across my driveway, I came face-to-face with the enormous beast. Okay, bobcats are not *that* big, and they have surprisingly small tails, but they are scary and intimidating up close and portray themselves like enormous beasts. Trust me!

The humongous, vicious carnivore was about fifteen feet away and staring right at me. I had no idea what to do. I thought, *If I just keep staring at it, I'll get my face clawed off. If I turn and run, I'll get clawed from behind. If I climb a tree, I'll get clawed up a tree.*

It seemed like getting clawed was inevitable. I was about to pee my pants when I thought, *Well, since I've got nothing to lose, I might as well call his bluff.* So I roared.

I gave him my best adult-Simba lion-king roar, and, by the grace of God, he turned and ran away. And I thanked Jesus for protecting my "a girl at a party once said it kinda looks like Tom Cruise's" face and ran into my house like a little kid.

I was not ready.

But I managed to escape unclawed.

When it comes to temptation, we're not usually so fortunate.

Think about the first time you gave in to temptation. Now consider the last time you gave in to temptation. The first time might've been lying to your parents. The most recent may have been deceiving your spouse. In between you've probably caved to temptation 47,340 times. (That's a rough estimate. Don't be offended. My personal count is considerably higher.)

What do they all have in common?

You were not ready for the temptation.

Jesus said, "Watch and pray so that you will not fall into temptation. The spirit is willing, but the flesh is weak" (Matt. 26:41).

Watch.

Pray.

Jesus teaches us to be spiritually aware of our weakness.

The apostle Paul encourages us to "be on your guard; stand firm in the faith; be courageous; be strong" (1 Cor. 16:13).

It's time to make up our minds to do that.

We are going to think ahead and be ready.

Why?

You Have a Spiritual Enemy

You have a spiritual enemy who is coming for you.

Go back and read that sentence again, because it is horrifying. We like to ignore the idea of the devil or make Satan into a fictional character in a red suit we can joke about.

But he is real.

And he is coming for you.

In the Bible, Peter warns us, "Be alert and of sober mind. Your enemy the devil prowls around like a roaring lion looking for someone to devour" (1 Peter 5:8). (That's the NIV; here's my version: "Be alert and of sober mind. Your enemy the devil prowls around like a serial-killer bobcat looking for someone to claw to death.")

Jesus said in John 10:10 that the devil is trying "to steal and kill and destroy" everything that matters to God.

You matter to God.

So the devil wants to destroy you.

Your spiritual enemy is strategic in his approach.

He studies you.

He knows your weaknesses.

He plans to attack where and when you are vulnerable.

So it is imperative that we watch and pray "in order that Satan might not outwit us. For we are not unaware of his schemes" (2 Cor. 2:11).

Most people don't plan to avoid sin. But you are not "most people." You are going to pre-decide to be ready "so that you can take your stand against the devil's schemes" (Eph. 6:11).

You Are Your Own Worst Enemy

Sorry to break it to you, but you are more sinful than you think you are.

Lest you think I'm judging—I am more sinful than I think I am too. We're more prone to wander and turn our backs on God than we're comfortable admitting. We don't like to think of ourselves as sinful, but "if we claim to be without sin, we deceive ourselves and the truth is not in us" (1 John 1:8).

That's why we can't afford to lie to ourselves about ourselves.

Because if we do, it makes us less ready and therefore more vulnerable.

In James's description of the process of temptation I previously shared, he writes, "Each person is tempted when . . ." Do you remember what comes next? We might guess, "Each person is tempted when [Satan comes in with his evil lies.]" Or "Each person is tempted when [they live in a godless world and are exposed to all its wickedness.]" But no. James writes, "Each person is tempted when they are dragged away by their own evil desire and enticed." According to James, you are your own worst enemy.

You're more sinful than you think you are.

And you're not as strong as you think you are.

We tend to think we can handle more than we can. That's dangerous. It's why we're warned, "Pride goes before destruction, a haughty spirit before a fall" (Prov. 16:18) and "So, if you think you are standing firm, be careful that you don't fall!" (1 Cor. 10:12).

Studies show that people overestimate their ability to resist temptation; the technical term for this is "restraint bias."[9] We are not able to control impulsive decisions and behaviors like we think we can.

This is why when someone brings their famous home-baked chocolate brownies to the office, you think, *No way. I'm not cheating on my diet. I will walk right past it!* And you do—the first time. The second time you cut a little sliver, just to taste it. The third time you walk by, not only do you eat a big piece but you somehow end up with chocolate in your hair.

What happened?

You thought you were stronger than you really were. That pride led you to rely on your limited willpower and, ultimately, to fall.

So why do we overestimate our ability to battle temptation?

We don't understand the energy it demands. Fighting temptation is fatiguing. The part of our brain that controls our willpower has other responsibilities too. It also helps us cope with stress, monitors emotions, and makes decisions. As we mentioned in the introduction, decision-making is a muscle that gets fatigued from overuse. Here is what that means:

> Your willpower will wane and wear out.

This explains why you do such a great job not saying what you want to your annoying coworkers but then go home and yell at your spouse. Or why you can be so disciplined and productive all day long, and then, once you get home, get nothing done. It's because willpower wanes. Self-control is a limited resource. The more we use, the less we have.

We're more sinful than we think we are.

And we're not as strong as we think we are.

So we have to get ready.

We don't wait to get ready when the moment of temptation arrives. Remember, that moment is fraught with peril. We're not great in the moment. So we're going to make three pre-decisions that will help us be ready when temptation attacks.

Move the Line

If I ask you what comes to mind when I say "Michael Jordan," you probably think "basketball."

I say "Warren Buffett," and you think "money."

I say "Helen Mirren," and you think "acting."

So when I say "Samson," what do you think?

The answer should have been this: *Oh, wow. He's, like, the Bible's superhero! Awesome strength. Incredible hair! Amazing opportunities to serve God and protect people.*

But that's not the answer. Samson is not actually a hero in the Bible. He's a cautionary tale. He's an example of what not to do.

Why?

Because Samson put the line in the wrong place.

Samson's story starts with his parents dedicating him to the Lord and God blessing him. He has massive strength and is a strong leader who confronts people who do wrong. Then it all goes off the rails.

Samson falls in love with Delilah, who was a Philistine. She asks Samson to tell her the secret of his great strength. Samson messes with Delilah, telling her he can be tied with "bowstrings." She has men come and tie him with whatever those are, but he easily breaks free.

Delilah complains to Samson that she feels foolish and wants to know the truth. *Um, time to break up, Samson?* But no, he continues to toy with her, claiming he can be tied with new ropes this time. Delilah has Philistines come and rope him up, but that doesn't work.

Delilah is mad, again. *Kinda suspicious by now, don't you think, Samson?* Once again, no. He tries to calm her down by telling her if his hair is braided, he'll lose his strength. So while he sleeps, Delilah weaves his gorgeous locks, but that doesn't work either.

When Samson wakes up with his hair braided, you'd think he'd say, "We're done! But can I still share your Netflix account?" But he doesn't. Delilah has now officially worn him down with her persistence. He's running out of clever answers. The strong man is about to show his ultimate weakness—character.

Samson finally tells Delilah the truth, revealing his secret that his hair should not be cut. So she has the top barber of the Philistines come to give Samson a fresh cut while he is asleep. When he wakes up, the soldiers take him captive, gouge out his eyes, and lead him to a dingy prison cell.

As Samson sat blind and shackled, you know he had to ask, "How in the world did this happen to me?"

Been there?

That's the question I asked when I woke up the morning after on my road trip and looked at myself in the mirror.

We ask that same question when our lives turn out nothing like we'd hoped.

How in the world did this happen to me?

The answer for Samson is the answer for us.

It's where we move the line.

Think about Samson's story.

Why was he even interested in a Philistine woman?

God had forbidden his people from marrying outside of their faith. And the Philistines weren't just outside his faith, they were the enemies.

And what's up with the hair, Samson?

His entire life Samson knew that the secret of his great strength was not to cut his hair. But when Delilah, an enemy Philistine, asked Samson how to take away his strength, he eventually told her the secret about his hair.

Samson knew there was a line—"Don't marry someone outside your faith" and "Don't cut your hair"—but he chose to walk as close to the line as he could, and when the moment came, he couldn't resist the temptation and fell into sin.

Think back to the last few times you caved when tempted. I bet it started by walking too close to the line.

Just like me. I never should have gone to the party. But when I did, I never should have listened to those girls. Then I never should have had that first beer. I went to the line, crossed it, and kept going. I know exactly what it feels like to wake up with a bad haircut, so to speak.

Few people plan to wreck their lives. But even fewer people plan not to. Again, you are not most people. Instead of being unwise, unaware, and unalert, we are making up our minds to be ready for the moment of temptation.

We are pre-deciding to move the line.

What Can I Do with Her?

When I started dating Amy, I was a new Christian. Before Amy, I was not a Christian and had no physical boundaries when dating someone. But I quickly discovered I was supposed to honor God with my body and wait until marriage for sex. I knew what I couldn't do with Amy, I just didn't know what I could do.

I went to a Christian guy I respected and asked. "Braun, what can I do with Amy?" I knew he knew the answer, but I tried to help him along. "Just, you know, gimme everything possible. Like, can I touch her? And if so, what can I touch? Details. I need details. Can I smell her hair? I can certainly smell her hair, right? Tell me everything I *can* do, Braun."

I was looking for the line. The line between right and wrong. Between acceptable and unacceptable. Between what God was okay with and what he wasn't. I didn't want to sin, but my intention was also to get as close to that line as possible.

I think most of us do that.

Yet we never do that when it's obvious there is real danger.

Right?

If a doctor is about to do surgery on you, you don't ask him, "How close can you get to my artery without slicing it and causing me to bleed out on your table?"

Or when I was studying to get my pilot's license, I never asked myself, *I wonder what's the least amount of fuel I can put in the airplane and still not crash and die short of the nearest airport?* If I'm looking at the map and see a two-thousand-foot tower, I never wonder, *How close can I fly to that tower without hitting it?* Of course not.

When it's obvious there's real danger, we stay away from the line.

But when it comes to sin, the danger is often hidden. It's like a fish seeing a juicy worm floating just below the surface of the water. Looks delicious! What it doesn't see is the hook in the worm that will lead to the fish's death.

What we see looks great!

What we don't see will destroy us.

The danger of sin is hidden, but it is there. That's why we feel comfortable cozying up to the line.

After I talked to Braun and started dating Amy, I soon realized if I got up close to the line, I'd end up going over it. You know what I'm talking about. The line that always gets blurry when you are out alone, way too late, playing her favorite love song on repeat. There was no way, in a moment of temptation, that I would be able to walk the line. Right? Her hair simply smells too good.

This principle doesn't apply only to dating. And it doesn't apply only to me. And it's true not only of me. Whatever the temptation, whatever the sin, for all of us, we are in trouble if we get close to the line.

So what do we do?

We pre-decide.

We move the line.

We pre-decide to move the line.

We know we have a spiritual enemy who is coming for us. We know we're not as strong as we think we are. So instead of getting close to the line of sin, we're going to move the line farther away from sin. If it's wrong and it's tempting, we're not going to get close. We pre-decide to move the line to put distance between ourselves and the temptation.

> Why resist a temptation tomorrow
> if we have the power to eliminate it today?

Ask yourself, "What can I do to move the line? How can I put myself in a place where I can't be tempted or at least won't be able to easily act on the temptation?"

Perhaps you have the spiritual gift of spending money on Amazon. You have incredible skill in clicking that Buy Now button, and when you do, you feel the glory of God. The problem is you're spending too much money. You bought some books, a shirt, the thirty-six-pack of toilet paper, the air fryer, the sushi roller, the lumbar support pillow, the Guac-Lock, the Boba Fett backpack, the burrito blanket, the ramen soup graphic hoodie, and a chicken harness.[10] You spend too much. You've thought, *I'm not going to buy anything else. I won't do it. I'm not gonna do it!* But then you did it, again. How do you stop?

You move the line.

For instance, you decide on a dollar limit per month or that you have to wait at least a week before ordering anything else. But if that doesn't work, you might have your best friend change your password so you can't click that magical Buy Now button unless your friend approves. That would move the line, and that would work!

Your issue may be spending too much time on social media. You're online for four or five hours a day. Sure, you have interesting friends, but not *that* interesting! You need to stop watching other people's lives and start living your own. You keep saying you want to stop wasting so much time, but you get sucked back into it every day. *Scroll. Like. Scroll. Comment. Double-click. Scroll.* So what should you do? Stop relying on willpower in the moment.

Instead, move the line.

You could go into your settings, choose the tempting app, and, if available in the advanced time options, set your limit for each day at thirty minutes.

If you're single, your issue might be that every time you go to a club, you get drunk and hook up. The next day you feel ashamed and swear you won't do it again. *The next time I go to the club, I will not get drunk and I will not hook up!* But then you go out and it happens again, and again, like your own self-destructive, tortured version of the movies *Groundhog Day* and *The Hangover*. How do you finally stop?

You move the line. You don't go to the club.

You know you're in trouble with sports betting, online gambling, or the lottery. Your 401(k) withdrawals or credit card bills are getting out of hand. Every time, you swear it's the last time. How do you finally stop?

You have to get the issue outside of yourself. You have to move the line by reaching out for help.

You know you cannot handle that temptation, so you refuse to put yourself in that position.

You pre-decide to move the line.

You might hear all of that and think, *Sure, that would work. But, well, it just feels so restrictive. I can't make a purchase without getting my friend involved? I'd have a limit on my social media time? I can't go to the club? I can't buy a scratch-off? Where's the fun? It feels like so many rules.*

Wrong.

You might miss out on a fleeting moment of pleasure here and there. But you'll save yourself from feeling the guilt and regret (not to mention the payments and the hangovers). You will save your finances, your productivity, and your integrity. You won't have to live in shame. You'll take your life back.

God created our lives to run free in his will the same way a train can go fast and far on a track. No one who looks at a locomotive flying by at a crossing thinks, "Wow, what a waste that such a powerful machine has to stay confined to those tracks." The train finds its freedom on the rails, built specifically to maximize its power and purpose. Just like our lives in God's plan.

I love what David writes in Psalm 16:6: "The boundary lines have fallen for me in pleasant places; surely I have a delightful inheritance." The lines God puts in my life, the boundary lines that keep me from disobeying him and living a less-than life, are *not* restrictive.

They're not limiting.

They're freeing.

It's time to move the line.

1.4

Magnify the Cost

We talked earlier about the devil whispering to us. Have you ever noticed that before you sin, he often tells you things like this:

- Hey, everyone else is doing it.
- It's really not that bad.
- It's no big deal.

Before you do something wrong, your spiritual enemy minimizes the consequences. But after you give in to temptation, the devil magnifies your sin by inducing feelings of guilt and shame.

- How could you do something so horrible?
- God won't love you now.
- People can't trust you.
- You are a worthless, pathetic person.

Solomon offered some very practical wisdom in Proverbs 27:12, the verse I first introduced at the beginning of part 1: "A prudent person foresees danger and takes precautions. The simpleton goes blindly on and suffers the consequences" (NLT).

Wisdom tells us the devil is a liar and always on the attack. So we anticipate temptation and pre-decide to take precautions.

For example, when I married Amy, I made a promise to her and to God that I would be faithful.

But all kinds of temptations trip up people who want to be faithful to their spouses. There's the trap of lust, now more pervasive than ever because of the internet. There's the trap of attraction to or the feeling of chemistry with another person. And we all know too many people who have fallen to those temptations and wrecked their marriages and their lives. It happens so often that it might start to feel difficult, or even impossible, to avoid.

So what do you do?

You magnify the cost.

We ask, "What could go wrong? What is the worst-case scenario, and what if it really happens?"

On the Roof

In 2 Samuel 11 we read how King David was hanging out on his roof.

Why was he up on the roof?

He was supposed to be with his men, fighting in a battle, but he had decided to stay home. Alone. That's why he was at his palace, but why was he on the roof?

We learn that, from the roof, David could see a beautiful woman bathing. You have to wonder whether David had been to this "website" before. Perhaps he knew about the line of sin that existed on his roof and could've moved the line ("I don't go up on the roof, ever") instead of getting close to it ("I need some fresh air, and the roof sounds good").

But David did not move the line. He ignored it.

He went to the roof and saw the woman, whose name was Bathsheba, and it occurred to him: *I could invite her over for a nightcap. I mean, I am the king. She'd like that, right?*

In that moment of temptation, what should David have done?

That's the wrong question.

We know that the best odds of success are not in the moment of temptation but before that moment ever arrives. Again, why would we resist a temptation in the future if we have the power to eliminate it today?

So what should David have done before facing the supercharged, adrenaline-fueled, dopamine- and norepinephrine-inflamed moment of seemingly unbeatable temptation?

He should have magnified the cost.

In the moment he was probably thinking, *I'll have her over. We'll just talk. It'll help us both pass the time. She's probably lonely with her husband at war. She'll be pleasant company and nice just to look at. She'll enjoy the honor of being a guest at the palace. Who wouldn't want that? That will be the end of it. No harm. No foul.*

But before the moment he could have asked himself, *What could go wrong? What is the worst-case scenario, and what if it really happens?* If he did, he might have realized:

- *We could end up having sex.*
- *I could wreck Bathsheba's life.*
- *She could get pregnant.*
- *I could attempt to cover up the affair by killing her innocent husband.*
- *My staff could see my sin and question my devotion to God.*
- *My military leaders could find out, damaging my integrity and respect as the nation's leader.*
- *I could suffer months of guilt and feel separated from God.*
- *The baby could die.*
- *My other children could rebel.*
- *It could bring tragedy on my family for years to come.*
- *The story could be recorded in history so my shame would be exposed to millions and become part of my legacy.*

Obviously, David did not play out the worst-case scenario.

He should have, because it became the *actual*-case scenario.

If he had pre-decided to magnify the cost, he wouldn't have been on the roof in the first place or he could have looked away if he did see Bathsheba.

What Could Go Wrong?

I don't want to make the same mistake David did, so I magnify the cost. My pastor used to quote Numbers 32:23 to me. "Craig, if you sin," he would say, "you will be sinning against the Lord, and you may be sure that your sin will find you out."

He was right. So I ask, "What could go wrong? What is the worst-case scenario, and what if it really happens? What could happen if I chose to be unfaithful to Amy?" This is difficult to think about. It's even more difficult to type on a page. But here goes.

- I would hurt God.
- I would lose the trust and respect of my best friend, the woman who has stood by my side and honored me with more love than I could ever describe.
- My six children, their spouses, and my grandchildren would no longer look up to me as a man of God.
- I'd lose the respect of thousands of people who trust me as their pastor. In a moment of stupidity, I'd surrender all my credibility and any spiritual authority to help them grow closer to Jesus.
- Five minutes of sin could wreck a lifetime of pursuing Jesus.

So I have pre-decided to magnify the cost.

It keeps me off the roof.

How about you? Have you asked yourself what could go wrong? Because it will go wrong. What's the worst that could happen if you get too close to the line and, because of temptation, trip over it?

- Your sin will come out. It always does.
- You could lose your reputation, your ministry, and your integrity.
- You could lose your job or a loved one.
- You could wreck your finances or your marriage.
- Your kids could resent you.
- Your spouse could leave you.
- If you persist in sin, you could miss your destiny.

Temptation never whispers any of that. But it's true. It's where temptation will lead you if you let it.

But we won't.

We are going to be ready, through the power of pre-deciding.

You are going to move the line.

You are going to magnify the cost.

And you are going to plan your escape.

1.5

Plan Your Escape

You are going to plan your escape.

A story was told in an 1897 magazine article about Sir Arthur Conan Doyle, the author of the classic Sherlock Holmes novels. To test the theory that everyone has "a skeleton in the closet," he sent an anonymous telegram to a church's revered archdeacon that read, "All has been discovered! Flee at once!" The story goes that the man disappeared and was never heard from again.[11]

True or not, the point is clear. Throughout history, millions of people have made their escape after sin has been found out, or even threatened to be. But we're going to flip this script.

You will decide—in advance—how you will get out of a temptation.

We see this in the Bible with Joseph.

His brothers had sold him into slavery, and he ended up working for Potiphar, the captain of Pharoah's guard. In Genesis 39, we're told Joseph was "well-built and handsome" (v. 6). You might say he was like Ryan Gosling. My wife would say he was like Craig Groeschel. (At least that's what I pretend she says.)

Because he looked so much like me, I mean Ryan Gosling, the Bible says, "After a while his master's wife took notice of Joseph" (v. 7). She made a move on Joseph.

Potiphar's wife doesn't even try to be creative. She takes the direct approach. "Come to bed with me!"

Wow, very different from David's story, huh?

Imagine how easy it would have been for Joseph to give in. Unlike David's situation, this could have been easily hidden by the official's wife. He could have justified sinning by thinking like this:

- *I didn't do anything wrong, and my brothers sold me into slavery. So I deserve a little fun.*
- *This is not my homeland. I'm all alone. No one will find out.*
- *I'm young. I'm single. She made the move on me. So maybe I should go for it.*
- *God hasn't done what I want him to do, so why should I do what he wants me to do?*

I always tell my kids, Don't use your disappointments to justify your disobedience.

But it's easy to do, isn't it? Have you been there? "My spouse isn't meeting my needs, so I gotta do what I gotta do." "My boss isn't paying me enough, so I'm going to find ways to get a little extra for myself."

Joseph could've justified saying yes to Potiphar's wife, but he had made up his mind to honor God with his life. So when she came on to him, he said no. Joseph told her he couldn't sin against her husband or against God. He had pre-decided the outcome long before the heat of the moment. He had moved the line to avoid smelling her hair.

He resisted. Then what happened? He was never tempted again, right? *Yeah, right.* She kept getting up in his business every day. Day after day she made her moves. Just like day after day the devil will come for you. Because we know our enemy is attacking, we're going to be ready. With God's help, we will plan our escape.

That's what Joseph did. Some might think he was strong for resisting temptation. Wrong. Remember, none of us are that strong.

Joseph wasn't strong.

He was ready.

He was wise enough to plan his escape.

One day Potiphar's wife approached him, and instead of using more words, she grabbed Joseph by his coat and tried to rip it off him. What did he do? Did he think, *Well, I guess this is finally the time I give in to temptation*? Nope. He turned and ran. He left his coat in her hand and escaped out of the house. He knew that it's better to have a good name than a good coat. He knew that a lifetime of honoring God is better than a few minutes of pleasure.

So he pre-decided: *If she grabs, I run.*

The Way Out

We need to do the same. When we're tempted, we often feel like we have no choice. We feel too weak and the allure seems too strong. When you feel vulnerable, remember, "God is faithful; he will not let you be tempted beyond what you can bear. But when you are tempted, he will also provide a way out" (1 Cor. 10:13). The NASB version uses the word "escape"—"But with the temptation will provide the way of escape also."

God provides a way out, and we need to run to it. We're told to "flee from sexual immorality" (1 Cor. 6:18) and to "flee the evil desires of youth and pursue righteousness, faith, love and peace" (2 Tim. 2:22).

We don't just fight, we flee.

And we don't just run haphazardly. We decide our escape route, in advance, for any temptation we see coming in the future.

The next time you go to a movie theater, pay attention to the moment when the lights go out and it gets dark for the film to start. Somewhere in the room you'll see a small rectangular sign that lights up with the word "Exit." While we never pay any attention to those, if an emergency occurred, that sign would show your path to safety.

When you get into a situation and suddenly everything gets dark, God promises to light up his exit for you, your sign to safety. To live a life of pre-decision, learn to look for his signs before the lights go out.

Attack of the Killer M&M's

Let's say you're trying to eat healthy. You open the cabinet and there's a big bag of M&M's. What do you do?

1. Go ahead and eat them. (They are delicious.)
2. Open the bag, throw all of the M&M's into the air, look up with your eyes closed and mouth open, and assume that if any M&M's fall into your mouth, it must be God's will that you eat them.
3. Follow your pre-decided escape route.

I want to suggest that number 3 is the only effective plan. And I would ask, If M&M's would be a temptation for you, do you have an escape plan? (M&M's are a real temptation for me. Superman has kryptonite. My kryptonite "melts in your mouth but not in your hands.")

So if I'm vulnerable to eat what I shouldn't, I need to decide in advance what to do. I pre-decided to ask for help. When I'm tempted, my escape route is to call a friend. I know sin grows best in the dark, so I bring it into the light. When sin is exposed, it loses some of its power. So I call someone. That person can pray for me and provide accountability by asking later what I did with the M&M's after I hung up.

If you're thinking, *Really, Craig, all of that to just not eat some candy?* Yes—because I'm serious about my health, even for what some may consider no big deal, I have pre-decided with an escape.

When you're tempted, God is always faithful and will never let you be tempted beyond what you can bear. He will give you an escape every single time. So we pre-decide:

- Move the line to avoid the temptation altogether.
- Magnify the cost, so the temptation loses its luster.
- Map out our escape, so if we are hit by a temptation, we know exactly what we'll do.

Why? Because no one plans to screw up their life, but people do it all the time.

The problem is that they didn't plan not to.

So we are going to pre-decide not to.

Your Weak Spot

Your spiritual enemy is not ineffective or indiscriminate. He has a strategic plan aimed to hit you where you're weakest.

Because that's true, you need to know where you're the weakest. Where are you most vulnerable?

What sin do you justify?

Is it pride?

Do you compromise financially because you look for your security in money or love the bling cash can bring?

Do you lie to make yourself look good?

Or manipulate people?

Do you gossip about others to make them look bad and you look better?

Do you judge? Are you overly critical?

Are you carrying unforgiveness in your heart?

Do you compromise your integrity when you want to fit in?

Do you find yourself giving in to lustful temptations?

Do you take God for granted? You were once passionate about him, but today you're lukewarm.

Whatever it is, you'll want to be ready, because your enemy is. He's ready to attack you at your weakest spots. If he hasn't yet, he will. If he already has, then you can be sure he will again. Just like Potiphar's wife, he'll keep coming at you.

So be ready.

I told you that I'd determined to be faithful to Amy for the rest of my life. I have friends who had the goal to be faithful to their spouses but, sadly, have not achieved it. That made me realize I am not above falling to temptation. So what did I do?

I moved the line. I decided ahead of time to eliminate anything that might be tempting or could give the appearance that I'm being tempted. The things I've done include the following.

I am never alone with a person of the opposite sex. (Some people criticize that. Feel free. My wife appreciates it and that's all that matters.)

I don't travel alone.

All of my devices—computer, iPhone, iPad—are locked down and transparent. I have the adult-content block on. A bunch of people have my passwords and can monitor what I have looked at. People see every written conversation I have on social media, texts, or email. I cannot download an app. Seriously. Someone else has to do it for me. It can be frustrating. I once tried to rent a hot-air balloon for a trip with my son. I couldn't because "hot" was in the search. But I would rather miss out on a hot-air balloon ride than wreck my life in a moment of weakness.

I am ready.

I know the devil is going to attack.

I know I am more sinful than I think I am and not as strong.

So why would I resist a temptation in the future if I have the power to eliminate it today?

The devil is coming for you. He's going to try to steal your joy and peace, kill your marriage and friendships, and destroy your reputation and witness.

So watch and pray. Be on your guard.

Because you are not as strong as you think.

So before moving on to the next section, let me encourage you to slow down and let the weight of what we've covered sink in. Consider asking yourself a few questions. Please have the courage to answer honestly.

- Where am I weak?
- Where am I vulnerable?
- Am I doing something I'd be embarrassed for others to know about?
- Where am I too close to the line?
- What is the worst that could happen if I continue in the direction I'm going?

Remember, you are only as strong as you are honest.

For you, this could be the moment of truth.

What are you going to do about what the devil is trying to do to you?

Pre-decide to move the line.

Magnify the cost.

Map out your escape.

And thank God that, at this very moment, he is giving you a way out.

PART 1 EXERCISES

1. What are you doing that you hate that you do? Where is temptation continually leading you to sin?
2. From your previous answer, what is being whispered to you? Be specific.
3. Have you misunderstood the difference between temptation and sin? Explain.
4. How could pre-deciding what to do (option C on p. 20) help you in your fight (option A) not to give in to temptation (option B)?
5. In considering Satan as a real threat you should take seriously, do you feel like your understanding of him is cultural (what people say), denominational (what your church says), or biblical (what the Bible says)? Explain.
6. Is there any place in your life where your pride in your willpower is keeping you from escaping temptation? Explain.
7. Considering your answers so far, where are you flirting with crossing the line and where do you need to move the line to save your life?
8. Using my example on p. 35 of magnifying the cost of sin, take your biggest temptation and create your own list. Then use what you write to help you pre-decide.
9. Now that you have learned to magnify the cost, take that same temptation and map out your escape route. Be specific about what to do.
10. Consider making it an ongoing discipline to take any regular temptation or sin and apply these three steps:
    - *Move the Line.* Write out specific action steps for how you will move the line.
    - *Magnify the Cost.* Write out a list of worst-case results to magnify the cost.
    - *Map Out Your Escape.* Write out the steps of your escape route.

I Will Be Devoted

They devoted themselves to the apostles' teaching and to fellowship, to the breaking of bread and to prayer.

—ACTS 2:42

What Lies Beneath

When Amy and I were first married, we purchased a really small home built in 1910. The only two closets in the entire house were shoebox size. We moved in and hung a few shirts and pants in each closet. That was it. No more room. We put a couple of pairs of shoes in each closet, which maxed out the floor space. Uh-oh. What about our big bag of dog food, board games, photo albums, VHS tapes (this was the early 1990s), rollerblades (again, early '90s), toilet plunger, winter clothes, and coats?

No problem. Our little house had a little basement, which we used as storage for everything.

It worked great!

Until our first big rainstorm.

You've heard the expression "It was raining cats and dogs"? Well, it was raining Great Danes and bobcats. (Not really, but my incident from the driveway causes me to see bobcats everywhere.)

We'd been out for the evening, and after a cautious drive through torrential rain, we made it home. When we walked into the house, we found our basement flooded with three feet of water. Our real estate agent had neglected to mention that the basement flooded several times a year. We looked and saw, to our dismay, floating dog food and board games and photo albums and rollerblades.

I leaped into the torrent and found myself standing waist deep in water. Our toilet plunger floated by. I considered grabbing it so I could start plunging, but I didn't know where to start. That's when Amy, peering safely from four steps up, reminded me that the previous owners had left a sump pump in the basement. I felt around until I found it. I pulled it out of the water and looked around for an outlet. I noticed the end of an extension cord dangling from a rafter directly overhead.

Hmm. I needed the sump pump to work. The sump pump required power to work. As I was still standing waist deep in the water, I knew this could be problematic, but the connection had to happen.

Had. To.

I thought, *If I plug this in really, really quickly, maybe I won't get shocked.*

So I said a quick, wet prayer and pressed the two metal prongs of the pump cord into the corresponding slits in the extension cord.

When they connected, power happened. I know power happened because my body became the pathway for billions and billions of teeny-tiny electrons. Electric power surged through the cords and into my body. Apparently the piercing shock triggered certain neurons in the language center of my brain where a long-unused word—a very bad word—was stored.

Milliseconds later, the sheer force of the electric current pushed the foul word toward the front of my face and out of my mouth. Unfortunately, it did not come out quickly. Probably because of the gazillion volts of electricity surging through my body, it came out at an unusually increased volume and seemed to last as long as an episode of *The Bachelor*.

I looked up and saw the horror on my new wife's face. Her preacher-husband had just shouted the mother of all bad words. I also saw fear—I think she believed I was about to die, and that word would be the last thing I ever said.

Part-Time Follower

You know how my house had an issue under the surface that the real estate agent hadn't acknowledged? Well, *I* had an issue under the surface that I hadn't acknowledged.

To be very clear—the bad word was not the problem. It was just embarrassing, outward evidence of the real, inward problem. Deep down, like in my basement, I knew there was something seeping into my heart and starting a flood that could create an even bigger issue sooner than later if I didn't deal with it. In that shocking moment, I got a wake-up call.

I realized that when it came to my devotion to God, I was simply "going through the motions."

As followers of Jesus we know we're supposed to prioritize him. You may have seen it on your friend's Instagram bio: God first.

But it's not just a cool thing we put on social media and T-shirts, it's in Scripture. It doesn't just appear in the Bible, it's a major theme. In the book of Matthew alone, we find Jesus saying:

- "No one can serve two masters. Either you will hate the one and love the other, or you will be devoted to the one and despise the other. You cannot serve both God and money" (Matt. 6:24).
- "But seek first his kingdom and his righteousness, and all these things will be given to you as well" (Matt. 6:33).
- "Jesus replied: 'Love the Lord your God with all your heart and with all your soul and with all your mind'" (Matt. 22:37).
- "Anyone who loves their father or mother more than me is not worthy of me; anyone who loves their son or daughter more than me is not worthy of me. Whoever does not take up their cross and follow me is not worthy of me" (Matt. 10:37–38).

Why should we put God first? Well, it's kind of like a car. The manufacturer tells you to put gas in the gas tank. We don't question, "What's your problem? Why do you insist on my putting gas in the gas tank?!" We understand that's the way a car works.

How *you* work is to have God at the center of your life. You put God "in your gas tank" by putting him first. If you don't, you will always feel empty. And always seek more.

If you don't put God first, nothing else will work right. Have you ever buttoned a shirt and by mistake put the first button in the second buttonhole? You keep buttoning, then get to the end and realize, *Wait a second. Everything is wrong.* Your shirt is totally screwed up. Why? Because if you put the first button in the second buttonhole, every button thereafter is in the wrong place. And if we don't put God first—if we put something else in that top spot—everything else ends up wrong and you find yourself wondering why your life feels screwed up.

If you don't put God first, you'll put something else first, and nothing else can handle the pressure of being the most important thing in your life.

- If you make your job the most important thing, your job will always disappoint you.
- If you make your marriage the most important, your marriage will struggle.
- If you put your kids and their success first, they'll be burdened by the weight of that pressure and will probably disappoint you.
- If you prioritize being happy, you will forever be disappointed, because you won't be able to achieve true, lasting happiness without God.

First is too much pressure to put on anything else. God knows that, so he invites you to put him first.

And I wasn't putting God first.

Yes, I was a Christian. And yes, I was a pastor. But somehow, somewhere along the way, instead of being faithfully devoted to pursuing Jesus, my devotion devolved to duty.

I still read the Bible, but only to prepare sermons.

I still prayed, but mostly in public during church services.

While I was waist deep in electrified water, God revealed something to me that stopped me in my tracks. He didn't speak audibly. But what I felt seemed louder than audible. God showed me this:

I had become a full-time pastor and a part-time follower of Christ.

Instead of being devoted to Jesus, I was devoted to pleasing people and looking "spiritual" and being a "good pastor." I was devoted to doing what *I* wanted to do.

But I wasn't fully devoted to Jesus.

Can we pause here?

I'd like to give you a moment to reflect on and honestly answer this question:

Are you faithfully, passionately pursuing Jesus?

Are you seeking him first? Are you pursuing him with whole-hearted devotion? Or are you a bit more like I was?

You might realize that you are a full-time mom and a part-time follower of Christ. Or a full-time student but only partially devoted to Jesus. You could be fully invested in your business, your fitness routine, your YouTube channel, or your freakishly stylish appearance, but you are not fully devoted to the one who is fully devoted to you.

In this moment of honesty, you may discover that you are not as committed, not as close, not as intimate with God as you once were. Or you might acknowledge that you've never really walked closely with him, sensing his loving presence, his ongoing guidance, and his supernatural power.

Why do we want to be devoted but find it so challenging?

When you think about it, the answer may seem obvious. No one ever gets close to Jesus by accident. Right? Has anyone ever said this:

- I didn't mean to, but somehow I'm stronger spiritually today than ever before.
- I'm not sure what happened, but all of a sudden I know God's Word and sense his presence.
- I was just doing my own thing, minding my own business, and suddenly I've become full of spiritual power and confidence in Christ.

We will never accidentally get close to Jesus, so instead we will choose to think ahead and pre-decide:

I will be devoted.

Because of who God is and what he has done for me, I am willing to do anything and give up everything for him. God is first.

God deserves that. Because God is God.

When you understand who God is, nothing else makes sense but to put him first.

I. Will. Be. Devoted.

What a Devoted Life Looks (and Doesn't Look) Like

My family moved a lot when I was growing up. As the new kid, I wanted to be cool. To be cool, you need cool friends. So I would go into my new school like a detective, looking for clues to ascertain which kids measured up.

When I was in fourth grade, I wanted to know, "Do you watch *Happy Days*?" The answer was critical. Don't give me no *Laverne and Shirley*. I wasn't down with "Schlemiel! Schlimazel!" or "Hasenpfeffer Incorporated." I was all about "Sunday, Monday, happy days!"

In sixth grade I would not so subtly ask, "Do you have Atari?" If you answered yes, you'd get the all-important follow-up question, "What's your fave game, bro?" I wanted to hear *Pitfall!*, *Donkey Kong*, or *Asteroids*. "What was that? *Ms. Pac-Man*?" No. If Ms. Pac-Man is your girl, then I ain't your guy. Ms. Pac-Man had a bow in her hair! (Well, she didn't have hair, but she had a bow where her hair should have been.) To me, Ms. Pac-Man was a clue you weren't cool.

In eighth grade the sign that you were cool, or not cool, was the bands you loved. If you listened to Guns N' Roses, "Welcome to the jungle, dude, we're gonna be buds, 'cause you *are* cool." But if you were a fan of Bananarama, that was clear evidence you were not cool, because good bands are never named after fruit!

That's how I decided whether you were cool.

Question: How do we know whether we're devoted?

Signs of Non-Devotion

People who are not truly devoted don't think about God a whole lot and tend to turn to him only when they need something. He's kind of like the drive-through at the fast-food restaurant. It's not really on your mind, but you're glad it's there when you need it. You're grateful it's available for you to pull up quick, order what you want, then speed away until you need it again.

Those who don't put God first

- crave acceptance from people more than acceptance from God;
- prioritize pleasing people over being faithful to Jesus;
- rarely share their faith in Christ with people who need him;
- give only when it's convenient (if they give at all);
- do whatever they want, then rationalize their sins;
- take God for granted, turning to him only when they're in a bind; and
- focus more on this life than on heaven, knowing that this life lasts only seventy-five to eighty years while eternity is forever.

They aren't very different from the rest of the world. They listen to the same music, watch the same movies, use the same language, have the same morals, raise their kids and approach their marriage and parenting in the same way.

Signs of Devotion

When I was a kid, I wanted to see if you had the signs of being cool. What are the signs of being devoted?

Where Your Mind Goes

What do you tend to think about repeatedly throughout the day?

There are things we think about more than others would. It might be fantasy football, the stock market, this season of *Dancing with the Stars*, or the dream of winning the lottery. Why? Because when you're passionate about something, you think about it.

Paul challenges every disciple to "set your minds on things above, not on earthly things" (Col. 3:2).

So how often do you find yourself thinking about God throughout the day?

Where Your Money Goes

We spend our money on what we care about. Jesus says, "For where your treasure is, there your heart will be also" (Matt. 6:21). The way you spend your money reveals your priorities. If you spend a lot of money on clothes, you're into fashion. If you spend a lot on concerts, you're into live music. If you spend a lot on your *High School Musical* or New Kids on the Block figurine collection, you're weird. So how much do you "spend" on God? If you are not generously giving back to God, not investing in his kingdom in a big way, that's a sign he's not truly first in your life.

How You Make Decisions

Let's say you were offered a new job that would require you to move to a different city. What criteria would inform your decision? Most would consider the salary and whether it's a place they want to live. People who are devoted to God seek his will. They try to discern where God wants them and where they might have the greatest impact for his kingdom. Or, if you're single, who will you marry? Devoted single people want to find a special someone who is attractive and fun and has a great personality, but above all they want to meet someone who also puts God first.

In Romans 12:2, Paul offers a path to the right mindset as we make decisions: "Do not conform to the pattern of this world, but be transformed by the renewing of your mind. Then you will be able to test and approve what God's will is—his good, pleasing and perfect will."

How You Spend Your Time

What if I told you that my wife means everything to me, that she is the most important person in the world to me, but then you found out I spend virtually no time with her? You'd be confused. You might think, *But if you cared about her, you'd spend time with her.* Yep.

And people who care about God spend time with him. They hunger for his presence, so they prioritize praying and reading the Bible and worshiping. They also invest time in what's close to the heart of God. They care for people. They volunteer in the church. They live to be a blessing.

Once again we can learn from Paul's teaching about how we use the time we are given: "So then, be careful how you walk, not as unwise people but as wise, making the most of your time, because the days are evil. Therefore do not be foolish, but understand what the will of the Lord is" (Eph. 5:15–17 NASB).

What Breaks Your Heart

When you devote yourself to God, your heart grows for him, and it breaks with the things that break his. You grieve over your sin. You forgive quickly, because you feel not only your pain but also the pain of the person who hurt you. You care for the poor, have compassion for outcasts, and desire to see injustices righted.

In Matthew 25:34–40, when Jesus teaches about the judgment, he draws his dividing line according to this dynamic.

> Then the King will say to those on his right, "Come, you who are blessed by my Father; take your inheritance, the kingdom prepared for you since the creation of the world. For I was hungry and you gave me something to eat, I was thirsty and you gave me something to drink, I was a stranger and you invited me in, I needed clothes and you clothed me, I was sick and you looked after me, I was in prison and you came to visit me."
>
> Then the righteous will answer him, "Lord, when did we see you hungry and feed you, or thirsty and give you something to drink? When did we see you a stranger and invite you in, or needing clothes and clothe you? When did we see you sick or in prison and go to visit you?"
>
> The King will reply, "Truly I tell you, whatever you did for one of the least of these brothers and sisters of mine, you did for me."

Jesus wasn't saying that good works will get you into heaven, but that when you are close to him, you will be involved with the people and places where he is present. Why else would someone feed the poor, take care of strangers, and visit prisons? And then do these things so often that they had to ask which time he was there! One thing is for sure, a disciple won't be able to focus on ministries like these for very long if their heart is not aligned with God's.

What If?

What if you are not devoted to God? You won't grow, you'll miss out on more of God and more of the life he made you to live, and all of it will leave you feeling empty and wondering what's missing.

What if you are devoted to him? You'll grow in purpose and spiritual confidence and become more and more like Jesus. Your life won't be perfect, but you'll know you're loved perfectly by a perfect God and that you are going to a perfect place to be with him. You'll find he keeps you in perfect peace as you trust in and fix your thoughts on him.

What if you are not devoted, but you want to be?

You can be. And, good news, although you need to make the pre-decision, living it out doesn't depend on you.

2.3

The (Shocking) Power of Connection

Remember when I was standing waist deep in my basement and found what I needed? The sump pump. But having the sump pump was not enough; I had to connect it to power. When I finally did, it worked. (And my limbs went numb. And my heart may have stopped for a second. But the pump did work.)

Devotion to God is what we need, but it's not enough. We need to connect that devotion to power. When we finally do, it will work.

You Are the Branch

We've acknowledged that full devotion to God will never happen by accident. That's why we have to pre-decide:

I am going to seek God first.

I mentioned Matthew 6:33 earlier, but here I want to highlight Jesus' promise that if you "seek first his kingdom and his righteousness," then "all these things will be given to you as well." What "things"? In the verses just before that, he tells us not to worry about what we eat, drink, or wear. He says God will take care of our needs if we stay focused on his will. He provides us with the power to change as we pursue him.

So I will pursue Jesus with everything I have.

I will be devoted.

You make that decision, and then you're empowered to live it out through your connection with Jesus.

That's why he says, "Come to me, all you who are weary and burdened." He doesn't say, "Then try harder." Or "Then stop failing." No. Jesus says, "Take my yoke upon you and learn from me" (Matt. 11:28–29). He's telling us, "The life you want is through connection to me, so come."

He also says, "All you thirsty ones, come to me! Come to me and drink!" Again, we need to come to Jesus. And if we do, what will happen? Jesus says, "Rivers of living water will burst out from within you, flowing from your innermost being" (John 7:37–38 TPT). Just like I had rivers of electrons flowing within, you can have the power of Jesus flowing within. The answer is to come to Jesus.

Jesus makes this clear when he says in John 15:5, "I am the vine; you are the branches. If you remain in me and I in you, you will bear much fruit; apart from me you can do nothing."

He said he is the vine.

You are a branch.

A vine comes up from the ground. A branch grows off the vine and has a vital connection with the vine. If it stays connected, it'll get the nutrients needed and bear fruit.

If it's not connected to the vine, a branch can do nothing. It won't get nutrients. It won't bear fruit. A disconnected branch is dead.

It's not even a branch.

It's a stick.

Jesus says, "If you remain in me." *In me.* Jesus is inviting you to connect with him and, more than that, to live inside of him. "Remain" is translated from the Greek word *meno.* It can also be translated "abide." To abide means to live in. You may visit a friend's house, but you abide in your home.

Jesus is inviting you to live inside of him. To abide in him. He also says, "And I in you." He's asking if he can live in you. Jesus is offering you a profound, intimate, continual connection.

The word "remain" appears eleven times in John 15. Eleven times Jesus tells his disciples he wants them to stay connected, to continually live in him.

That's not what most Christians are doing. If you looked at their lives, it's not what you would see.

We can think of this in terms of hours. Our lives are made up of time. So let's think one week at a time. Each week you get 168 hours.

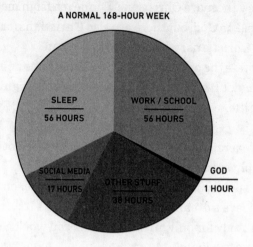

A NORMAL 168-HOUR WEEK

SLEEP
56 HOURS

WORK / SCHOOL
56 HOURS

SOCIAL MEDIA
17 HOURS

OTHER STUFF
38 HOURS

GOD
1 HOUR

If you're truly devoted to something, you'd devote time to it. Right?

So where do you spend your time in a normal 168-hour week? Most of us spend about one-third of our time sleeping.

Most spend another third of our time at work or school.

That leaves you about 56 flexible hours remaining.

What do you do with those hours?

Are you on Facebook, Instagram, TikTok, or X? The average social media user spends seventeen hours a week online. (Can you pause for a moment to let that sink in? Seventeen hours of your week!)

That leaves about thirty-nine hours for all the other stuff, and there is a lot of other stuff. Right?

You drive your kids around like an unpaid Uber driver. You have to put gas in your car every six or seven days, and clean the inside of your car every six or seven years. There's buying groceries and cooking groceries and eating groceries and cleaning up after you eat them. There's paying your bills every month and your taxes every year. And mowing your lawn. And working out. And hanging out with your friends. And binge-watching whatever TV series you're into at the moment.

And all of that takes about . . . *wait a second, I've got to use my calculator* . . . thirty-eight hours. Then thirty-nine minus thirty-eight leaves you . . . one hour.

What do you do with that hour? Well, we're Christians, so we give that hour to God.

Of course, there are Christians who devote significantly more than an hour a week to God, but there are also Christians (or people who call themselves Christians) who don't even do that.

Let me state the obvious: if you devote only one hour a week to anything, you're not likely at all to grow or improve significantly in that area of your life.

- If you exercise only one hour a week, you are not going to get in great physical shape.
- If you spend only an hour with your spouse each week, you won't have a dream marriage.
- If you study for only an hour a week, you won't get As. You may not even graduate!

If we give only an hour or two a week to God, no wonder we don't think about him much, fall back into the same old sin, care so much about what other people think, keep all of our money, and find ourselves with a lukewarm faith. So we need to ask ourselves some questions:

Are we really devoted?
Have we put God first?
Is he even anywhere close to first?

If we want to live a life fully devoted to Jesus, it will never happen by accident.

We need more—more connection so we have more power to live a more devoted life.

He is the vine. You are the branch. So be the branch!

Be the Branch

If we are the branches (as we stay connected and devoted to Jesus), he says we will "bear much fruit."

According to Galatians 5:22–23, spiritual fruit includes "love, joy, peace, patience, kindness, goodness, faithfulness, gentleness, and self-control" (NLT). Aren't these all things you want more of?

If you had more fruit, do you think your life would feel empty? Do you think you would be wondering if there is more to life? No. You'd be connected to Jesus and, through his power, living out your highest calling in the most meaningful way.

We want that.

God wants it for you.

But you have an enemy who will leverage every force in hell to keep you from it.

That's why you will be ready.

And you will be devoted.

2.4

Distracted from Devotion

The devil doesn't need to destroy you if he can distract you.

Yes, he wants to destroy you. He is coming for you to steal, kill, and destroy. But he knows if he can distract you, eventually you will destroy yourself.

His plan is to detour you from your devotion by distracting you from coming to Jesus, so you don't have the connection that can empower your decisions.

Have you ever felt that?

Pulling Apart

The word *distraction* stems from a Latin word of the 1590s. It meant "a pulling apart" or "separated."

You've felt *that*, right?

You've felt your attention and your mind being pulled in different directions.

- You want to think pure thoughts, but you're pulled away.
- You try to pray but find yourself spinning in a hundred other directions.
- You feel like you're getting separated from your connection with Jesus and devotion to God.

It's not an accident.

Every force of hell is working to distract you from living for what matters most. Your enemy wants to pull you apart, divide your mind, discourage your faith, and distract you from what matters most. That's why I tell my kids the devil doesn't need to destroy you if he can distract you. If he distracts you, he can enjoy watching you destroy yourself.

It's actually easier to distract you than destroy you.

Why?

Because to destroy you the devil has to get you to do something bad. You might be ready for that. But he can also distract you by getting you to do something good.

The Battle between Good and Best

Think of when Martha and Mary had Jesus over for a meal. Mary "sat at the Lord's feet listening to what he said. But Martha was distracted by all the preparations that had to be made" (Luke 10:39–40).

What was Martha doing?

Good things.

She was setting the table, checking to see if the casserole was done, getting the cobbler ready to put into the oven, asking if anyone wanted a refill on their drink, choosing a great Spotify station to create the right ambiance. Was any of that bad? No, it was good.

She was being a servant and taking care of people. My momma taught me that's what we should do.

Mary, on the other hand, was sitting around not helping at all. My momma taught me that's what we should not do.

But Jesus told Martha, "Martha, Martha, . . . you are worried and upset about many things, but few things are needed—or indeed only one. Mary has chosen what is better, and it will not be taken away from her" (Luke 10:41–42).

Martha was distracted by "many things"—all good.

They were good.

They just weren't best.

As Jesus said, "Mary has chosen what is better."

So often our most difficult choices are not between good and bad but between good and best.

That's why we need to pre-decide what is best.

To prioritize our devotion to Jesus, we have to diminish our distractions.

I love what Paul writes: "I am saying this for your benefit, not to place restrictions on you. I want you to do whatever will help you serve the Lord best, with as few distractions as possible" (1 Cor. 7:35 NLT).

I wonder what most distracts you from connecting with Jesus?

For a lot of us, it's our mobile device. Studies reveal the average person struggles to go ten minutes without picking up his phone and touches his phone 2,617 times a day.[12] Humanity went thousands of years without phones, but today our trinity has become Father, Son, and Holy Phone. Perhaps the most distracting thing on your distracting phone is social media. I mentioned the average person spends about seventeen hours a week on social media. That will amount to more than seven years of your life.

Stop.

Read that again. Don't just accept that stat as normal. Read it and let it sink in.

You will spend more than seven years of your life on social media.

Doing what? Scrolling, clicking, feeling left out because you weren't invited, comparing, feeling less than because you don't have what they have, feeling unimportant because someone doesn't comment on your pics but you always comment on theirs.

Is social media bad?

No.

It's often good. Okay. But it's not best. It is not the best use of your time.

I like social media, too, but I have decided this:

> My life is too valuable, my calling too great, and my God too good to waste my time distracted by things that do not matter.

Because our time is so valuable, and because Satan wants to destroy us by distraction, I'd suggest we need to treat distractions the same way we treat sin.

What do we do with sin? We move the line, magnify the cost, and map out our escape.

What distracts you from connecting with Jesus? Screen time with

TV, video games, or social media? Fantasy novels? Obsessively follow-ing the news?

Magnify the cost: if you continue to let yourself be distracted, it'll rob you of connection, which will destroy your devotion. You might be a part-time follower when God deserves your full-time devotion.

And then move the line and map out your escape.

What do you need to do?

- Turn off notifications?
- Delete that app?
- Put some distance between you and your gossipy friend?
- Cancel Netflix?
- Limit your time on social media or in front of the TV?
- Turn off your phone when you pray and read the Bible?
- Dump your distracting boyfriend or girlfriend?

Whatever it is, it will be hard, but worth it, because God has a path and a purpose for you. "Set your gaze on the path before you. With fixed purpose, looking straight ahead, ignore life's distractions" (Prov. 4:25 TPT).

You'll have to say no to some good things, but you will be saying yes to what's best.

Your Rule and a Game Plan

There are "rules" for life.

- Return borrowed vehicles with the gas tank full.
- Say please and thank-you often.
- Sing in the shower.
- Leave the toilet seat down. (That seems to be my wife's favorite.)
- Leave the space better than you found it.
- Never double-dip your chips.
- Offer to take your shoes off when you enter someone's home.
- At a door, allow people to exit before you try to enter.
- In a public space, don't talk loudly on a phone call or put someone on speaker.
- (Fill in the blank with one of your own.)

Those are some rules *for* life, but have you heard of a "rule *of* life"? Christians having a rule of life has been traced back to the year 397 when Augustine wrote a well-known "rule book" for Christians.

What is a rule of life?

It's a set of intentional rhythms that help us to do the following:

- stay connected to Jesus
- know him more
- become more and more like him
- create spiritual, relational, or vocational practices
- align our priorities, values, and passions with the way we live our lives

- overcome distractions, to not be so scattered and hurried and reactive and exhausted
- start living for an audience of one

Want to hear something fascinating?

Remember Jesus says he is the vine and we are the branches? If you look at a vineyard, you'll see the vine and the branches, and you'll see a trellis. The trellis is the support structure. Without a trellis the branches will just grow wild along the ground. But on the ground they're more prone to disease and more susceptible to pests that want to eat their fruit. Off the ground and supported by the trellis, the branches will grow healthier and produce more fruit. A trellis also makes for a more beautiful vineyard—instead of growing haphazardly along the ground, the vine and branches grow intertwined and vertically.

If you want healthy branches and a good crop of fruit, you need to provide a sturdy support structure.

So what's fascinating? The word for "rule," as in "rule of life," in Greek is the same word for "trellis."

Like a trellis, a rule of life creates a structure of spiritual practices. With this structure, instead of feeling chaotic, you live by a spiritual rhythm. You're healthier, less vulnerable, and more fruitful. You'll live a more beautiful, God-honoring, and people-loving life.

I want to encourage you to pre-decide your rule of life.

Your rule will probably include some practices that help you build your relationship with God, such as Scripture reading, praying, and fasting. It may include some practices that nurture your physical life, such as sleep or sabbath or exercise. You may have some relational elements that focus on your friendships and family. You should consider having some practices attached to your church involvement—attendance, fellowship, service, offerings. And you might include a work/vocation category.

There are plenty of articles on the internet and books that can help you develop your own rule of life, so for now I want to point you to just one essential spiritual practice:

Spend undistracted time with Jesus.

We know we won't accidentally spend rich and meaningful time with Jesus. So we will pre-decide to be intentional. Our strategy will include three things:

- a time
- a place
- a plan

In Mark 1:35 we're told how Jesus spent undistracted time with his Father: "Very early in the morning, while it was still dark, Jesus got up, left the house and went off to a solitary place, where he prayed." His time? Very early, while it was still dark. His place? Away from the disciples in a place of solitude. His plan? Focused and intentional solitude and prayer.

With Jesus as our example, because devotion matters, we will intentionally eliminate distractions so we can connect with him in a meaningful way through solitude, prayer, Bible study, personal worship, scripture memorization, or whatever allows you to come to Jesus and give him space to work in your life.

A Time

Jesus invites us to come to him and do life with him all the time. Yet most of the time distractions keep us from really focusing on him.

It's similar to a marriage. Amy and I will sometimes have a weekend when we're around each other most of the time. I love that. But, at the same time, there will be all kinds of distractions—there are other people around, we're running errands, the TV is on—so we don't connect in a significant way. That's why we need "couch time" or a date night. And we don't wait to see how the week goes, hoping we can fit in some time for each other. We prioritize that special focused time with each other.

If we want God to be first, we can't give him the leftover time in our day. We give him the best time in our day, every day. You'll want to find what time will be best for you. For many, it's first thing in the morning. You might spend time with Jesus before your kids get up, or as you drink your coffee. Or your best time to spend with Jesus might be after you go to the gym or after you get your kids in bed.

Your devotion to God is too important for this to be unintentional and erratic.

What's your time?

Let's name it. Prioritize it. Plan it.

You will determine a time for connecting with Jesus.

A Place

We're also going to choose a place.

It doesn't always have to be the same place—you may have some special days when you can go somewhere different. But, for the most part, having a consistent place to pursue Jesus will probably help you do this consistently.

You might kneel by your bed, or sit at your kitchen table, or go out on your back porch. If you have young kids, you may have to go into the bathroom and lock the door. Or maybe your closet. (And hurry, because it won't be long before you see little fingers sliding under the door.)

My suggestion? Choose a place you will love. Make it as comfortable, or as functional, or as attractive as possible. It's the most important thing you'll do every day, so do everything you can to help you want to do it. Create an environment you'd be sad to miss. Pick your favorite chair, put the chair by the window with the best view, wear your favorite robe. Have a cup of your favorite drink in your hand. If you like colors, buy a bunch of high-lighters or colored pens and use them to mark up your Bible or to journal.

This is the most important time of the day, so make it your favorite time of the day!

What's your place?

Let's name it. Prioritize it. Plan it.

You will determine a place for connecting with Jesus.

A Plan

Pre-decide a time, a place, and also a plan.

If something is important to you, you plan it out ahead of time. You might plan a first date, a vacation, or a special anniversary dinner. So instead of showing up at your time and place in a disorganized way and then feeling like you don't know what to do, you will pre-decide a plan. Your intention is to encounter Jesus. He has invited you into that time and you'll be open to whatever he wants to say to you or do in you. You will be flexible, but you'll develop a plan.

What plan? That's up to you. You might try one or more of these:

- Choose a YouVersion reading plan to study the Bible.
- Listen to a devotional podcast you love.
- Have a playlist of worship songs that draw you close to God.
- Choose a Bible memory app you can use to hide some strategic verses in your heart.

My wife has a journal in which she writes down the people she's praying for and what God is showing her. I have a reading plan I enjoy along with daily spiritual declarations to renew my mind.

The plan is up to you, but I encourage you to pre-decide a plan. What's your plan?

Let's name it. Prioritize it. Plan it.

You will determine a plan for connecting with Jesus.

A Branch Bears Fruit

As you start prioritizing this time with Jesus, something is going to happen. Your time with Jesus will start seeping out of your time with Jesus. You might spend those fifteen or thirty or sixty minutes with him, but as you do that day after day, your connection with Christ will grow outside of that time. You'll find yourself

- talking to and trusting him, depending on him, and aligning your heart with his;
- starting to hear his still, small voice as he nudges you throughout the day;
- receiving wisdom as he guides your steps;

- loving those who are difficult to love;
- forgiving those who hurt you;
- blessing those who curse you;
- having your heart break for what breaks his;
- becoming aware of your sin and turning away from what's wrong so you can pursue what's right and pure;
- generously sharing Jesus with others, as you are unable to keep his goodness to yourself;
- living by faith and seeing God do more in you and through you than you ever imagined.

And you will realize something's changed. Remember those fifty-six flexible hours?

God will no longer get your leftover hour or two. God will no longer feel like just a part of your life.

Instead, God is your life.

You'll discover that every hour of devotion you commit to him will have an incredible impact on all the rest of your 168 hours!

You'll start living the life you were meant to live, and you will realize it's happened. "I will be devoted" has turned into "I am devoted."

I am seeking first the one who matters most.

Get Your Affairs in Order

One day I received a text from an unknown number that essentially said, "Hello, this is Rhonda. I am Rodney's sister. Rodney is in the hospital with a rare form of progressive cancer. The doctor is not giving us much hope."

Rodney was a longtime friend of mine, so I rushed to the hospital.

Rodney was a big, strong athletic guy, but when I walked into the hospital room, the Rodney I saw was so frail it took me aback. I tried to act like I didn't notice, but I was thinking, *Oh no, this does not look good.*

It was difficult for Rodney to speak, but we started by doing the guy thing—we joked and laughed and told a few old stories. But the tone of our conversation turned serious very quickly. Rodney looked at me and began to speak, struggling for each word. "Craig," he said, then paused and took a big breath, "when the doctors tell you to get your affairs in order, you look at your life and think about the things you wish you had done."

His words hit me like a gut punch.

I asked and he shared some of his regrets. (His list was longer than I'd expected and hit me harder than I'd anticipated.) Then we joined hands and together prayed one of the most passionate, faith-filled prayers I'd prayed in a long time.

I said goodbye to my friend and left.

A week later Rodney's family and close friends gathered to celebrate his life and grieve our loss.

Listening to Rodney, hearing his regrets, made me look again at the 168 hours a week that add up to my life. I asked, again, *What matters? Who* really *matters? What is going to matter when this life is over?*

I thought, *I want to devote my life to that. I want to minimize the regrets I'll have when I'm the one lying in the bed in the hospital.*

I realized, again:

God is what matters.

God is God.
He is first.
I want to live my life devoted to him.

My intentions are good. But without intentionality, I will be distracted. I will lose my connection to the vine.

I won't be a branch bearing fruit.

I'll be just a dead stick.

I thought about how I struggle to live devoted, and I recommitted myself to staying connected to the vine.

I am just a branch.

I need to be the branch.

Together, let's decide to be the branch and to stay committed to the vine by pre-deciding a time, a place, and a plan.

We will be devoted. We put God first. We seek God first.

By the way, it may feel like that's a lot, like God is asking a lot of you. If so, there's something to remember. Yes, he is asking you to put him first. But God has already put you first. 1 John 4:19 says, "We love because he first loved us." God is asking you to seek him first. But he already sought you first. He's asking you to devote your life to him, but he first gave up his life for you on the cross.

God didn't just decide to do that.

He *pre*-decided to do that for you: "Even before he made the world, God loved us and chose us in Christ to be holy and without fault in his eyes. God decided in advance to adopt us into his own family by bringing us to himself through Jesus Christ. This is what he wanted to do, and it gave him great pleasure" (Eph. 1:4–5 NLT).

Back in eternity past, before he created the world, before there was a you, God pre-decided to seek you and have Jesus die for you.

Why?

Because he loved you.

Who is God?

He is the Holy One. The Lion of Judah. The Lamb of God.

He is my Source. My Strength. My Sustainer. My Shield.

He is all good. He is completely pure. He is perfect, without fault, without blemish.

He is the Holy One.

My God is infinite, immutable, immeasurable, incomprehensible.

He is self-existent, self-sustaining, self-sufficient. He has wisdom he didn't need to learn. He has strength he didn't need to earn. His ways are higher. His plans are better. His love is deeper than our finite minds can comprehend.

Some may choose to ignore him, leave him, or despise him. I choose to stay. To honor him. To treasure him. To love him.

Why?

Because of who he is.

I am devoted to him.

I know you want to be too. Not part-time. But giving your full devotion to the One who gave it all for you. Besides, who else can save you? Who else can heal you? Who else forgives your sins? Who else can comfort you in your pain? Who else will never leave you, no matter how bad it gets? Who else will always be for you? And if he is for you, who can be against you?

You're not going to find love like that anywhere else.

God is devoted to you. He put you first.

Let's put him first.

I am devoted.

PART 2 EXERCISES

1. What people, things, or situations do you tend to put before God?
2. Why do you think the answers you just wrote down often get the top spot before God?
3. Do you feel like you're a part-time or full-time follower of Jesus? Explain.
4. For each of the five signs of devotion to God, write down your thoughts, struggles, and strengths to honestly evaluate each area:
   - Where your mind goes.
   - Where your money goes.
   - How you make decisions.
   - How you spend your time.
   - What breaks your heart.
5. Consider your previous responses and answer the following questions:
   - Where is your strongest devotion?
   - Where is your weakest spot?
   - How can this insight help you grow and mature your devotion to God?
6. What tends to distract you most from spending time with Jesus? (Think through your relationships, possessions, and activities.)
7. What distractions do you need to get rid of by treating them the same as sin, by moving the line, magnifying the cost, and mapping out your escape? Be specific with the actions you can take.
8. Name some "rules of life" that you can pre-decide to give your spiritual life more structure and produce more fruit. (Examples: Scripture reading for spiritual health; exercise for

physical well-being; more family time and church fellowship for quality relationships.)

9. To prioritize and plan an undistracted time with Jesus, what will be your best time, place, and plan?

10. What are some ways you have seen your intentional time with God affect the rest of your 168 hours? If you haven't yet experienced this, how do you think such a commitment might affect you?

11. Understanding that God is devoted to you and puts you first, what is one step of devotion you can take toward putting him first?

I Will Be Faithful

Well done, good and faithful servant!
You have been faithful with a few things;
I will put you in charge of many things.

—MATTHEW 25:21

3.1

One Word

If you could choose a one-word goal to describe your life, what would it be? Let's say this word represents your character and summarizes what you stand for and have achieved.

There are so many options.

I did a little informal survey, and three of the most common responses were these:

- successful
- influential
- happy

No surprises there. I get that.

Those are good choices, but I believe there's a much better one. A word that should be at the front of our minds and top of our hearts. A word that should motivate us each day and inspire us to live for what lasts.

Why am I so convinced this is the best word?

Because when we get to heaven, if we have lived a life that pleases God, he's not going to say, "Well done, my good and successful servant," or "Well done, my good and influential servant," or "Well done, my good and happy servant." I'm guessing God wants us to be successful, influential, and happy, but I don't think they're his top priorities. When we get to heaven, if we've lived a life that pleases him, God will say, "Well done, my good and *faithful* servant" (Matt. 25:21 NLT).

So if you could choose a one-word goal to describe your life, what would it be? There are many options, but none is better than *faithful*.

If, in the end, that's what God will be looking for and commending, let's think ahead to that all-important moment and pre-decide, right now:

> I will be faithful.

When you were a kid, you had other goals in life. It's likely you wanted to grow up to become an astronaut, ballerina, professional athlete, firefighter, or social media influencer. You didn't say, "When I grow up, I want to be faithful!" But now that we've grown up, it's time to refocus our lives.

We're pre-deciding to be faithful because we will never be faithful by accident. You may have a fluke day of faithfulness, but no one is faithful day after day after day without great intentionality.

Why?

Because we love what's easy. But being faithful is rarely easy. Right? It's never difficult to cut corners, fudge the truth, or take the easy way out. But living with integrity, doing what's right, and honoring God consistently takes a lot of work (and a lot of help from God). Compromising our values is convenient, but there's always a cost. Faithfulness, on the other hand, is rarely easy. People may laugh at you. You might feel left behind. It may be harder than you expected. But remember this:

> Faithfulness honors God. And God honors faithfulness.

If you are faithful, it will be difficult and you will pay a price, but it will be worth it.

To be faithful we will need to learn to trust God instead of relying on ourselves. Habakkuk 2:4 tells us, "Look at the proud! They trust in themselves, and their lives are crooked. But the righteous will live by their faithfulness to God" (NLT). In our prideful self-dependence, we often trust in our wisdom, our knowledge, our goodness, our abilities, or our bank account. But Scripture says that those who trust in themselves have crooked lives. They don't walk a straight, faithful path; they veer off because of unfaithful decisions. So, because we are prone to pride, we pre-decide not to trust ourselves but to trust God and live in faithfulness to him.

This raises a question: What does it mean to be faithful?

If you had asked me years ago, I would've said, "It means you don't cheat. You don't cheat on your spouse, cheat on your taxes, use cheat codes on video games." There is truth in that, but as I studied how Jesus talked about faithfulness, I realized it has far more depth than I realized. It's just as much or more about the dos as the don'ts.

If you study the Gospels, you'll see that Jesus talks about faithfulness in three specific contexts. He talks about faithfulness in how you treat people, how you steward resources, and how you respond to God. So we are going to make three faithful pre-decisions:

1. Every interaction is an opportunity to add value.
2. Every resource is an opportunity to multiply.
3. Every prompting is an opportunity to obey God.

Good news: you may not be an astronaut, pro wrestler, or YouTube star, but with God's help and some prayerful pre-decisions, you can be faithful.

3.2

Every Interaction Is an Opportunity to Add Value

If you're anything like me, there is someone you're thinking about every time you interact with someone else. Yourself.

We are ridiculously focused on ourselves.

Think you're not?

How about this: If someone takes a group photo of you and seven other people, who is the first person you look at when you see it?

You.

If you look good, is it a good picture?

Yes.

What if you were having the best hair day and your sparkling smile was perfect, but everyone else had their eyes closed and one person was midsneeze? (Midsneeze is the purgatory of photography.)

It's still a great picture. If you look good, you approve, no matter how anyone else looks.

What if you're blinking, or have food in your teeth, or look twenty pounds heavier than you really are, but everyone else in the photo looks their personal best?

Delete the picture. Now.

And if your friend doesn't delete it and instead posts it? Not your friend anymore! They obviously never loved you in the first place.

If this were just a matter of pictures it wouldn't be a big deal, but we take that same self-centered approach into most of our interactions with people. We tend to think like this:

- *What does this person think of me? Do they like me?*

- *Do they approve of my clothes? My style? My conversation? If so, why didn't they mention anything about it?*
- *Did I say the right thing? Should I not have said that?*
- *I need to let them know how I feel about what we're talking about. This whole conversation is kind of pointless without my opinion.*
- *What am I going to get out of this?*

That is the natural way people think, but we don't have to live a natural, self-centered life. Because the Holy Spirit lives inside of us, we can live a supernatural, others-focused life.

> We can follow Jesus in living beyond the norm.

And so, because of our desire to be faithful, we pre-decide that every interaction is an opportunity to add value. It's what Jesus did and what we're called to do, as it says in Ephesians 4:29: "Do not let any unwholesome talk come out of your mouths, but only what is helpful for building others up according to their needs, that it may benefit those who listen."

What if every time you walk into a room, your intention is to improve the climate?

What if every time you interact with a person, your purpose is to be a blessing?

We always look to meet a need or be an encouragement.

What Jesus Did

Why should we meet needs and encourage others? Because we follow Jesus, and that's what he did.

When Jesus met a leper, he didn't ignore his need. He touched the man everyone said was untouchable and healed his leprosy.

When the disciples worried about what was going on around them, Jesus didn't play into their fear. "Yeah, you should worry. I mean, you should totally worry! With this political party in charge, and the economy? Did you see the news today? And what about Caesar's latest tweet?" No, instead Jesus told them, "So do not worry, saying, 'What shall we eat?' or 'What shall we drink?' or 'What shall we wear?' For the pagans run after all these things, and your heavenly Father knows that you need them. But seek first his kingdom and his righteousness, and all these things will be given to you as well. Therefore do not worry about tomorrow, for tomorrow will worry about itself. Each day has enough trouble of its own" (Matt. 6:31–34).

Jesus viewed every opportunity as a way to encourage, to meet a need, to share God's grace.

In John 6, when Jesus tried to get away, but hungry crowds followed him, did he turn his back on them? No, he supersized a kid's Happy Meal and fed everyone an all-you-can-eat bread and fish buffet.

In John 8, when a woman who was caught in her sin was brought to Jesus, did he say, "Shame on you. I can't believe you did such a thing!" No, Jesus looked at her with compassion and asked, "'Woman, where are they? Has no one condemned you?' 'No one, sir,' she said. 'Then neither do I condemn you,' Jesus declared. 'Go now and leave your life of sin'" (vv. 10–11). He didn't give her what she deserved, he gave her freedom.

In John 18, when Peter denied knowing Jesus, not once, not twice, but three times, did Jesus cancel him? Did Jesus say, "Peter, I can never trust you again," or "I'll forgive you, but I'll never forget what you did." No, Jesus forgave Peter and, by chapter 21, told him, "Go, feed my sheep." He restored Peter as a spiritual shepherd and gave him a place of leadership.

Jesus loved Peter.

Jesus added value, encouraged people, met needs, and shared his grace with everyone.

And Jesus blessed Peter with the greatest healing and restoring force in the universe through the unconditional goodness of God.

What We Do

That's what Jesus did, and as his followers, we make up our minds to do the same. We view every interaction as an opportunity to add value.

- We show grace.
- We meet needs.

- We forgive.
- We build up.
- We bless, serve, and speak words of life.

If you are faithfully following Jesus, this is what you do too.

Linda Wilson-Allen was featured in a front-page article in the *San Francisco Chronicle*. Is she a celebrity or politician? No, Linda Wilson-Allen is a bus driver.

A reporter for the *Chronicle* took her bus every day, and he was confused by what was happening. Why? Because Linda knows all of the regulars, calls them by name, and waits for them if they're running late and not at the stop when she gets there. One day he watched Linda get off the bus to help an elderly woman who was struggling with heavy grocery bags. (He thought, *Bus drivers don't do that.*)

Another day Linda discovered a woman who was new to town. She invited her over for Thanksgiving. (He thought, *No one does that.*) He watched, day after day, as Linda loved and blessed and served people exactly as they needed. The journalist requested an interview and asked Linda to explain how she was able to consistently have such a loving attitude. He wrote in the article what he learned: "Her mood is set at 2:30 a.m. when she gets down on her knees to pray for thirty minutes."[13]

Pastor John Ortberg interviewed Linda at his church. He asked about her 2:30 prayer time. Linda described how she asks God to show her what he wants to put in front of her. "It could be someone less fortunate than I am, to give them some shoes. . . . He'll show you. That's where my kindness comes from."

The pastor asked if, after she prays in the morning, she continues to pray while she's on the job, driving the bus. She replied, "Yes, when I'm out there doing my job ministering, I call it ministering."

Most people would call it "getting a paycheck," but Linda Wilson-Allen considers every interaction an opportunity to be faithful to God by being a blessing to people.

God calls us to do the same. It's not about what we do for a living, it's about what we pre-decide to do as we live.

When we choose to be faithful, we have no idea how God might use even a single word of encouragement to change someone's life.

I am a living testament to that; it's the reason I'm in ministry today. You may have heard me share this story before, but because it was such a game changer in my life at such a crucial crossroads, it's worth repeating.

When I was a young pastor, my whole life revolved around serving Jesus in the church. When I first applied for ordination, I was certain they would recognize God's calling on my life. Instead, to my utter shock, they rejected me. I'll never forget the moment the spokesperson for the group told me, "We just aren't sure you have what it takes to be a pastor."

My life felt like it had just crashed.

I may have been the only person in Oklahoma ever turned down for ordination by this denominational group that I mistakenly thought was desperate for more pastors. It was humiliating. After getting the news, I drove back in my little red Geo Prizm crying my eyes out, mostly because I had been rejected (but partly because I was driving a Geo Prizm).

When I got back to my church, I threw myself onto my pastor's desk sobbing. Nick Harris, my pastor, looked at me (well, he looked at my back; my tear-stained face was smothered into his desk) and said, "Craig, please listen. Craig, please listen to me." I stopped bawling and turned to listen. "Craig, no man can stop what God calls you to do."

That's why I do what I do today.

All of the impact I've had for God has flowed out of those ten words.

Nick loved me.

Nick added value.

Nick was faithful to God and spoke light into my darkness.

God worked through Nick to speak life to me and keep me on track with my calling.

You can be a "Nick" to the "Craigs" in your life. With God's help, you can be faithful to him by viewing every interaction with others as an opportunity to love and add value. Think about it:

- God put you in the place you live so you can love your neighbors for him.
- God gave you the job you have so you can be a blessing to your coworkers, clients, and customers.

- God can use you on social media to "do everything without complaining and arguing, so that no one can criticize you. Live clean, innocent lives as children of God, shining like bright lights in a world full of crooked and perverse people" (Phil. 2:14–15 NLT) as you are "holding out to them a Message of Life" (Phil. 2:16 WNT).
- God gave you friends who need hope.
- God will show you a single parent who needs help.
- God will put someone in your path today who needs healing.

You can love them.

You can add value.

If you do that, you will be faithful.

And you have no idea how God can use your faithfulness in other people's lives.

3.3

Every Resource Is an
Opportunity to Multiply

A Word and Its Opposite

Have you ever played the word association game? Someone gives you a word and you respond immediately with the first word it makes you think of. It might go like this:

Bubble.	Bath.
Apple.	Pie.
Phone.	App.
Chicken.	Egg.
Cow.	Milk.
Dog.	Bark.
Cat.	Run.[14]

You can also play a word *opposite* game when you try to quickly come up with the exact opposite of a word. So it could be like this:

Beautiful.	Ugly.
Truth.	Lie.
Day.	Night.
Government.	Efficiency.
Cat.	Harmless.[15]

Most "dis-" words have a natural opposite. Like the opposite of *disconnected* is *connected*. The opposite of *disagree* is *agree*. The opposite of *dislike* is *like*. But, curiously, some "dis-" words have no opposite version.

You can be disheveled—which means messy—but you can't be sheveled. Why?

And I will admit I've been disgusted a few times in my life, but I have never been gusted, nor have I heard someone say, "Man, that's so awesome, it really gusts me."

Then there's the odd *disgruntled*, in which the prefix "dis-" is not a negative but an intensifier. If you are disgruntled, you are really gruntled! But what does it mean to be gruntled? Nothing today, but back in the day it meant to grunt (or grumble or complain).

Another word that curiously has no opposite: *reckless*. Someone who is reckless acts without considering the consequences. Yep, got it. But can someone who thinks carefully before acting be called "reckful"? Nope.

About now you're wondering, "Okay, Craig, do you even have a point here?"

Believe it or not, I do.

I want to get you thinking about the meaning of *faithful* and what might be its opposite.

You Get a Bag of Gold! And *You* Get a Bag of Gold!

If we were to play the word association game and I said *faithful*, what word would come to your mind?

What if I asked you for the opposite of *faithful* and I said you couldn't answer with "unfaithful"?

I think we can get some help from a story Jesus told about a man who gave away bags of gold like Oprah gave out cars to audience members.

Jesus tells this parable in Matthew 25 about a man who is about to go on a journey. Before the man leaves, he entrusts his wealth to his servants. That is interesting to me. When we go on trips today, we don't leave our money with our friends. I guess our modern-day equivalent might be leaving your dog with a friend or having someone house-sit (which feels a little different from handing over $400 and saying, "Hey, watch this for me while I go to the beach").

This rich dude gives one servant five bags of gold, another two bags of gold, and a third just one bag. (The whole thing gives me Scrooge McDuck vibes. If the three servants were named Huey, Dewey, and Louie, I'd lose it.)

The first two servants go to work, strategically investing the money so they might have more to give when Rich Dude returns.

You can kind of imagine them

- watching *Dragons' Den* (you know, the precursor to *Shark Tank*) to look for new companies so they could jump on their IPO;
- examining some bond and annuity options;
- buying some Dogecoin and hoping for another big run;
- analyzing the price-to-earnings ratio of various stocks;
- debating whether Apple will continue to rise, or if that predicted swarm of locusts might lead to a bad crop of apples and lower the value of Apple; or
- wondering if they should invest in Olive Garden, which, at that point, did not have unlimited salad and breadsticks (back then, Olive Garden was just a garden of olive trees).

Whatever they decide, they make wise investments and both double what they were given.

When Rich Dude returns, he tells each of them, "Well done, good and faithful servant! You have been faithful with a few things; I will put you in charge of many things. Come and share your master's happiness!" (Matt. 25:21).

Notice they multiply the master's resources, and the word Jesus uses to describe them is *faithful*.

> Multiplying what you've been given in the kingdom of God is faithfulness.

The Greek word translated "faithful" is *pistos*, which describes someone who is faithful in the transaction of business, the execution of commands, or the discharge of official duties.

Watch the progression:

- The master entrusts his servants with resources.
- The servants multiply what they were given.
- The master calls them faithful.
- The master rewards their faithfulness with more resources.
- The faithful servants share in the master's happiness.

Before all of the blessings, the servants had to be faithful. And this is God's plan for you too.

One way you can be faithful to God is to care for and multiply what he's given you. *That's* faithfulness.

God's given you a yard? Make it a better yard.

God's given you a clunker of a car? Make sure you have the cleanest clunker of a car on the road!

God's given you a body? Take care of your body as best as you can.

God's given you some time? Use it to bless and serve others.

God has given you some money? How can you best steward it and multiply its impact for his kingdom?

That's faithfulness.

I've noticed that some Jesus followers who are in business can feel like second-class Christians because they're not in ministry. But being good in business is one of the most God-honoring things you can do. You are being faithful if you

- provide a product or service that adds value and blesses people,
- are an effective manager who leads with integrity,
- create jobs that provide for people and their families, and
- treat people well.

I'd argue you are being just as faithful when you do that as when you read the Bible or fast or teach a kids' class at church. Remember Linda, the bus driver? Don't tell the regulars who ride her bus that she's not in ministry!

> You are being faithful when you multiply the resources God has given you.

Jesus says *that's* faithfulness.

Word association: You say "multiply" and Jesus says "faithful."

So what's the opposite of being faithful?

Remember Rich Dude trusted three servants with his wealth. We've seen the faithfulness of the first two, but what about the third?

We're told he is afraid. He fears investing the money because he might lose the money.

It's easy to judge him, but I feel for the guy. I can think of times when I was afraid to make a mistake, especially with something I knew didn't really belong to me.

He is scared, so he hides it in the ground. When the master comes back, this servant digs the money out and approaches Rich Dude. After all of that digging, he is probably disheveled. (He certainly wasn't sheveled. Though he had recently shoveled.) He gives back all of the money—just as he received it.

What should the master say to him? Perhaps "Well done, good and faithful servant, you played it safe. You knew it wasn't your money, so you didn't risk losing it."

Nope.

Rich Dude is not gusted. He is disgusted, disappointed, and disgruntled.

He says to the third servant, "You wicked, lazy servant."

The other two were faithful. Why? Because they multiplied what they were given.

This servant is called wicked and lazy. Why? Because he did not multiply what he was given. Note: he did not lose any or steal a speck; there was no misappropriation of funds. The master calls him wicked and lazy simply because he did not multiply what he was given.

When I asked for the opposite of "faithful," the word "wicked" may have come to mind. But we learn here that to Jesus the opposite of faithful is lazy. When we are lazy with the resources God has given us, we are not faithful. It's wicked.

So what has God given you? How can you be faithful to him by multiplying every one of those resources?

3.4

Every Prompting Is an Opportunity to Obey God

Compelled by the Spirit

My wife, Amy, has a look.

When I say "a look," what I mean is that Amy has a very specific secret visual code language that she uses in public to privately tell me what I'm doing wrong without anyone else knowing that she's telling me.

Like I said, Amy has a look.

Unfortunately, when we were first married, I didn't speak her secret-look language. Why? Because I'm a guy. And guys can be clueless.

The first time I saw the look was when we were hosting a small group dinner party at our first house. I had just told a pretty funny joke everyone seemed to like. And when I say everyone, I mean everyone except Amy.

She gave me the look.

I was confused. Did she have something in her eye? Did she sit on a tack? Did dinner not settle well?

So I smiled awkwardly and told another joke that might have been even better than the first. Again, everyone thought it was funny. And by everyone, I mean everyone except Amy.

She gave me the look again.

Now, I may be slow, but I'm not stupid. It dawned on me, *Maybe, just maybe, she didn't like my joke.* So I backed off and changed the subject. Amy stopped giving me the look and bounced back to her normal happy self as if nothing had happened.

Now, after more than three decades of marriage to Amy, I have learned to decipher her coded messages. While I can't give away all our secrets, I can tell you she has not only a look but also a nudge, a tap under the table, a squeeze, a harder squeeze, and an "if you do that again you will regret it for the rest of your life" squeeze. Let's just say I've learned to discern what she wants me to know.

The same can be true with God. Our God is a relational God. Because he is relational, he loves to speak to us. He speaks to us in different ways:

- through his Word
- through circumstances
- through people
- through his Spirit

The good news is you can grow to learn to recognize God's voice speaking to you. Just like in a new marriage, it may take a little time to discern when it's God prompting or speaking to you. But the more time you spend with him, the more you sense his direction. And when God prompts, directs, or speaks to you, I promise you one thing: your response will take faith.

We see this in Acts 20. Paul was in Ephesus and happy to be there. But then he announced he was leaving for Jerusalem, saying he feared "prison and hardships" might be waiting for him there. He left his friends in tears. Why did Paul leave? He said he was "compelled by the Spirit" (Acts 20:22). The words in the original Greek are *dedemenos ego to pneumati*. While that sounds like what you almost ordered at the Thai restaurant the other day, it literally means to be wrapped up, as in to be bound with cords. Wow. Paul was like, "I can't explain it, but it's a leading from God, and I have to do it."

If you commit to following Jesus, he will lead you. He will prompt you, and faithfulness means feeling compelled to obey, even when you don't know what will happen next.

Obedience and Outcomes

Years ago, Amy and I were in a different part of the world. We did several days of ministry, then had a day and a half off. There was a beach about a thirty-minute walk from our hotel. Our first afternoon free, we walked to the beach and sat in the sand. For some reason I suddenly felt prompted to call my friend, whom I'll call Dave. I told Amy, "I feel like I'm supposed to call Dave."

She said, "Then call him."

But there was a problem. I told her, "My phone's back in the room."

Amy smiled and said, "Well, I guess you need to go back to the room."

I walked thirty minutes back to the room and called Dave. I had totally forgotten about the time zone difference, but it was midnight when the phone rang for Dave. He picked up and, instead of saying hello, abruptly asked, "Why are you calling me now?" That's when it hit me. "Oh, Dave, I'm so sorry. It's midnight there. I just felt a prompting to call you."

His voice quivered as he asked, "Why now?"

I knew he had been battling severe depression while going through an extraordinarily difficult time. So I asked as gently as I could, "Dave, are you planning on taking your life?"

"Yes, I am," he said. "I'm gonna do it."

I asked, "Do you have a gun? Do you have something in your hand right now?"

He whispered, "Yes, I have a gun and I'm going to use it."

Recognizing the importance of the prompting that led to the call, I said, "Do you realize that I'm in a different part of the world and God loves you so much that he prompted me to reach out to you at just the right moment?"

Dave sat in total silence.

I prayed he would realize how much I loved him. Even more, how much God loved him.

"God had me call you at the moment you needed him most. That's how much God loves you. Put down the gun, Dave. You're not doing this."

Dave started crying.

By the grace of God, Dave didn't take his life (and today tells everyone about the miracle story of God's perfect timing). I was stunned, again, at God's ability to use me if I'm just open to his leading.

> You have no idea what God might do when you faithfully follow a prompting.

Since I've pre-decided to be faithful, I try to always be open to God's promptings. But, probably like most people, I'm easily distracted from daily intimacy with him and can get stuck in more self-absorbed ruts. That's why I regularly tell God, "I'll do anything you prompt me to do. Just say the word."

Sometime later, I felt impressed that I should pray with my son Stephen the next time I saw him. I went home later that day and Stephen was there hanging out with a bunch of his smelly teenage friends. (I'm not being rude. They had just been on a run and smelled like Lazarus after four days of being dead.) Not wanting to embarrass Stephen or make it awkward, I told God, "I'll pray for him when his friends leave." But I felt like God nudged me and said, "No, go pray for him now." I hesitated. Yes, I am a pastor, but it felt really weird. What would his friends think? Why now? Totally out of the blue? But I wanted to be faithful, so I laid my hands on him, right in front of his friends. He looked at me funny. His friends looked at me really funny. I started praying for him, and I got a little emotional, then he looked a little emotional.

Finally I stopped praying. He looked at me. *They* looked at me. I walked off awkwardly. We haven't talked about it since.

So what's the miracle?

There is none.

Why tell you the story? This is why:

Obedience is our responsibility. The outcome is God's.

We want to be faithful, and that means pre-deciding that we will obey every prompting. Sometimes you'll see the reason for the prompting, but other times you won't.

Either way, we will be faithful.

When God puts someone or something on your heart, you will rarely be sure. *Is this God? Why would he ask me to do this?* But we have pre-decided. So you move forward in faith. You tell the person, very humbly, "I think I'm supposed to tell you," or "I felt like I should text you," or "I just felt led to bless you." The only way you will learn to follow God's prompting and grow in your faith is to step out and follow his voice.

We may be slow, but we're not stupid. So we pre-decide: I am faithful in obeying God's every prompting.

3.5

Free to Risk

Faith Requires Risk

Why would we ever say no to God?

We have three pictures of being faithful:

1. adding value to the lives of others
2. multiplying the resources you've been given
3. following Jesus as he leads you with his Holy Spirit

All of that sounds great, adventurous, fun, special. Right?

So why would anyone say no?

Risk.

If you seek to add value to someone's life, it will mean putting their needs above your own. When you do that, it feels like risk.

With multiplying resources, let's not underplay what went into the two guys' faithfulness in Jesus' parable. They were investing someone else's money with the possibility of losing it. They must have agonized in prayer, sought wisdom from others, analyzed their opportunities. After making the investment, they had to wait to see what happened, tormented by whether they made the right decision. All of that felt like risk.

When Paul left Ephesus for Jerusalem, where he expected prison and hardship, and when I walked through the group of my son's friends to pray for him, it felt like risk.

What will stop you from being faithful? Risk.

But faith in a big God allows you to take big risks.

It's more than that. Faith doesn't just allow you to take risks, faith is risk.

Faith *requires* risk.

Let me illustrate: If I were to yell up to you, "Jump off the roof. I'll catch you. You can put your faith in me!" what would it feel like? Risk! Why? Because it *is* a risk. Because you are being asked to put your faith in someone.

Or if I were to tell you, "Share your secrets with me. I know you've been burned by a lot of people in the past, but you can put your faith in me," that would feel like risk. Because it is a risk. It's a risk because you are being asked to put your faith in someone.

Faith is risk. It requires risk.

And God is looking for faithful people. People who will take risks. We're told, "Without faith it is impossible to please God" (Heb. 11:6). That means you cannot play it safe and please God. Contrary to bumper-sticker theology, following Jesus doesn't make my life safe. As my friend Mark Batterson says, "Jesus didn't die to keep us safe. He died to make us dangerous."

The wicked, lazy servant played it safe.

The two faithful servants played it dangerous.

A life of faith is a life of risk-taking. We see that with every person in the Bible who lived a life of great faith. Check out God's Hall of Fame in Hebrews 11. Every person is commended for his or her faith, and every person's faith required great risks. It's impossible to play it safe and please God.

Why does God want us to risk? Because he wants us to have a vital reliance on him, and he wants us to form a strong bond with him through that dependence. But if we play it safe, we don't really need God.

But, again, the problem is that risk leads to fear. I wonder if that's why one of the most repeated commands in the Bible is to "fear not."

We want to live risk-free, but God wants us to live free to risk.

Still, we'd prefer to play it safe. Why? Fear. Risk induces fear. It's hard to overcome fear. But we have to if we want to be faithful.

How to Overcome Fear

I want to teach you the key to overcoming fear so you can honor God with faithfulness. Whether or not you take a risk is generally based on the amount of fear it induces, but if you learn this secret, it can help you be faithful by giving you the courage to take risks you normally wouldn't. Ready?

Your willingness to risk is based on the potential return.

For instance, would you run into a burning house? No, you wouldn't. Why? Because it's a risk, and the fear of taking the risk would be too great.

Let's try another scenario. Would you run into a burning house if you realized your pet goldfish was inside? No, you still wouldn't. Why? Because it's a risk, and the fear of taking that risk is greater than the potential return of saving your goldfish.

But what if your child was inside? Would you run into the burning house? Yes, you would, without hesitation. It's the *exact* same risk and it would induce the same fear, but you would do it because the return is worth the risk.

The reason most Christians won't take the risks necessary to be faithful is because they stare at the risk and are stopped by fear.

- Why might a follower of Jesus not follow Jesus when he leads them to call a friend at midnight? The fear of looking stupid.
- Why do so many churchgoers never volunteer in their churches? Because of the risk of not being good enough or being overwhelmed by the extra time commitment.
- Why don't most Christians tithe? Because it feels like risk to live off only 90 percent of their salary.
- Why do 95 percent of Christians never share their faith? Because of the fear of being rejected by their friends.

When we stare at the risk, we're stopped by fear. But we can stare down the risk if we stay focused on the potential return. Lives are changed forever when we're generous with our money, when we follow the Spirit's leading, when we volunteer, when we share our faith. And when we do these things, we are being faithful.

It doesn't change the risk involved, but we can overcome our fear because we realize the return is worth the risk.

Have you ever watched the show *Chopped* on the Food Network? Each episode begins with four chefs who get eliminated one by one until the last remaining chef wins $10,000.

A few years ago there was an episode in which one of the chef contestants was named Lance.

From the beginning, Lance announced he was a Christian. He repeatedly mentioned that he was a follower of Jesus and how God had changed his life, and that he cooks for God and went on the show for God.

There was another contestant who explained that her grandmother lived in France, and she'd always been really close to her but hadn't been able to see her in a long time. Now her grandmother was about to die. She told everyone that if she won, she would use the money to go to France to see her one more time and say goodbye. You could see she was distraught about the whole thing, and at one point Lance the Christian offered to pray for her.

As the drama mounted, the contest came down to the two of them. And in the end Lance, the Christian, won.

The other contestant looked totally dejected and started to walk out. Lance called after her, "Wait!" She stopped, and he said, "You deserve to see your grandmother. I'm going to give you the ticket."

The girl stared at him, wide-eyed, as though asking, "Are you serious?"

Lance smiled and said yes, and the judges start crying. (And I may be getting a little misty-eyed just writing about his faithful sacrifice.)

He used his winnings to pay for her to go to France and be with her grandmother!

Lance was faithful and followed the prompting of Jesus. He made Jesus look amazing, which is perfect, because Jesus is amazing.

Why did he do it?

- It was an opportunity to add value to someone's life.
- It was an opportunity to multiply the $10,000 God had just provided him. He didn't actually lose the money, because he made Jesus look amazing to the millions of people watching the show. I'd call that multiplication!
- It was an opportunity to obey God after being prompted by him.

I'm guessing Lance felt a little fear and took a big gulp before he said, "Wait!"

But he knew the return was worth the risk.

3.6

Vastly Underestimating

People sometimes ask me, "When you started Life.Church, did you ever think you would affect so many people?"

The answer is no way. Not at all.

When we were planning to start the church, I met with a mentor of mine, Gary Walter, at Denny's for breakfast. Staring across his All-American Slam breakfast, he said to me almost prophetically, "Craig, I promise, you are gonna overestimate what you can do in the short run."

I looked at him kind of funny, but it ended up being true. After about a year our church had 120 people and I was disappointed. I wanted to reach so many more. I had prayed we'd affect our city in a big way, but it just wasn't happening as I'd hoped.

Gary repeated his first sentence for impact as he continued, "You are gonna overestimate what you can do in the short run. But you will vastly underestimate what God can do through a lifetime of faithfulness."

I'll never forget those words. And nothing anyone has said to me has been truer.

Can I share that same wisdom with you? You will overestimate what you can do in the short run, but don't lose heart:

> You will vastly underestimate what God can do through a lifetime of faithfulness.

So why, eventually, has Life.Church had an impact on so many people?

It's all God. But it's God using my thousands of decisions to be faithful, almost always in small things. Because when you are faithful with little, God trusts you with more (Luke 16:10). I'll give you a few examples.

I started dating Amy and we pre-decided to be faithful in purity and wait until we were married to engage in the gift of lovemaking. It was incredibly difficult for Amy. (Okay, no, it was difficult on me. *Really* difficult.) But we honored God in faithfulness.

Then on May 25, 1991, I made a promise to God and Amy to be faithful to her so long as we both shall live. To this day I have kept that vow.

When we were first married, Amy and I took a class on how to honor God with our finances. Even though we didn't have much to manage, we made three commitments to God. First, we promised to prioritize God in our finances by giving him back 10 percent. Second, we chose to invest 10 percent (which was not easy because we weren't making much). Third, we made the commitment to never borrow money for any purchase except a house. To say we lived modestly in the early years is an understatement. But God used what I learned personally to prepare me to manage more spiritually in the years to come.

In 1996, Amy and I felt prompted to start a different kind of church, believing one day God might do something special through it. We were scared to death at the risk we were taking, but soon we had forty people meeting in a garage and we had an anointed overhead projector. (Overhead projector? Google it.)

During that time I met a nineteen-year-old named Brian Bruss. "Brussman," as I called him, was one of the best waiters at Macaroni Grill I'd ever seen. There was something special about him, and I was honored to help disciple him spiritually and help him grow in his leadership. Now he adds value to the city of Norman, Oklahoma, because he is our campus pastor there.

In 2008 one of our pastors, Bobby Gruenewald, told me, "Hey, Apple's coming out with apps." I asked, "What's an app?" He explained it to me and said, "Why don't we start a Bible app? We could give it away for free!" I was terrified by the risk. How could we make an app? How would we afford to pay for it but not charge for it? But we felt the Spirit of God compelling us. That app was the YouVersion Bible, and we never could have imagined that we'd eventually give it away to well over half a billion people.

During the pandemic churches were closed, and we didn't know if people would ever come back. It was scary. We had planned on breaking ground for a building for a new location in Colorado Springs. It made no sense to spend the money to build a building in the middle of a shutdown with no idea what might happen in the future. But we sat in a little room and prayed and felt called by God to take a step of faith and break ground. Today, as I write this, more than two thousand people attend our church in Colorado Springs and hundreds of people have come to faith in Christ.

What's the point?

When you're faithful with a little, God will trust you with much.

Be faithful in each small thing. God will trust you with more.

1. Every interaction is an opportunity to add value.
2. Every resource is an opportunity to multiply.
3. Every prompting is an opportunity to obey God.

Your responsibility is to be obedient. Trust God with the outcome. You'll overestimate what you can do in the short run, but you will vastly underestimate what God can do through a lifetime of your faithfulness.

PART 3 EXERCISES

1. What is your one-word goal to describe your life? Explain.
2. What rooms do you walk into regularly in which God might be calling you to improve the climate? Write them down and explain.
3. Considering the people you regularly engage with, to whom might God be calling you to be a blessing? Write down their names and explain.
4. Think about the Christian bus driver in San Francisco. What are some practical ways you could approach your job or work as ministry, like she did?
5. Think about your family, friends, neighbors, and coworkers and make a short list of people you can more proactively love, as Jesus does. Consider how to add value to these relationships.
6. What one resource comes to mind that you know God is calling you to multiply for him?
7. Have you ever felt compelled to speak to someone or take action, and you saw God work through your faithfulness? Explain.
8. What is the biggest faith risk you have ever taken? What made it feel so risky to you?
9. Is there a risk you know God is calling you to take right now?
10. Where might you be underestimating what God can do in your life? Explain.

PART 4

I Will Be an Influencer

You are the salt of the earth. . . .
You are the light of the world.

—MATTHEW 5:13–14

4.1

Are You an Influencer?

Sadie Robertson is. Millions of people watched her on *Duck Dynasty* and *Dancing with the Stars*. As of this writing, she has 5 million followers on Instagram and 1.7 million on X.

In a convocation speech, Sadie asked a crowd of about twelve thousand college students, "How many of you would say you are an influencer?"

Only a few hands went up.

She explained that the definition of influence is to have an effect on someone's behavior or character. She made the case, "I think everyone's an influencer. Not everyone is famous. Everyone's an influencer.... We have twisted the word *influencer* in our generation."

She told the crowd that she wants to use whatever influence God gives her to point people to Jesus. "That is the most influential thing you can do in someone's life."

She taught the students that "it's the enemy who tells you you're not an influencer," because the truth is you can have more influence than you dare to imagine.

Sadie said, "The Word of God says you are called to be a light in the darkness. Not to be a little light that's hidden under a counter, covered by a blanket. No, don't hide your light. Be a 'city on a hill' kinda light.... Let's go to the darkness and shine it so bright."[16]

Pass the Salt. Shine the Light.

When Sadie shared that thought, she was echoing the words of Jesus, who says,

You are the salt of the earth. But if the salt loses its saltiness, how can it be made salty again? It is no longer good for anything, except to be thrown out and trampled underfoot.

You are the light of the world. A town built on a hill cannot be hidden. Neither do people light a lamp and put it under a bowl. Instead they put it on its stand, and it gives light to everyone in the house. In the same way, let your light shine before others, that they may see your good deeds and glorify your Father in heaven. (Matt. 5:13–16)

Who are you? You are salt. You are light.

What does salt do? It flavors food.

What does light do? It dispels darkness.

Take note: salt and light find their purpose when they come into contact with food and darkness.

That's why Jesus tells us, "Go into all the world and preach the Good News to everyone" (Mark 16:15 NLT). Go.

In 2021, Lifeway Research published the results of a survey of two thousand unchurched Americans; it reported that only 29 percent (three in ten) have ever had a Christian share their faith with them. But 79 percent of those interviewed said they don't mind their friends talking about faith, and 47 percent would be open to the conversation.[17]

This study shows that eight out of ten people who need the gospel don't mind hearing about it, and half of them are open to it! This blows the argument "they don't want to hear it" or "they aren't open to Jesus" out of the water.

Too many Christians today ignore the mission Jesus gave us to share our faith. Rather than reach out with love to those who are far from God, they keep their distance. But Jesus said, "Go into the world and shine," not "Go into your homes and hide."

Eats with Sinners

Years ago I was asked to lead a funeral, and a well-known businessperson in my city was in attendance. He was quite successful, but he was best known for his hard-partying lifestyle. He was wild. Evidently, the funeral touched him spiritually, because he called my office and told my assistant, "I don't go to your church and I'm not a religious guy, but I have some questions and I was wondering if Craig would meet with me." Of course, I said yes.

We met in the middle of the day at a restaurant that was so full they asked if we would mind sitting at the bar. My new friend said, "We'd be happy to sit at the bar."

It crossed my mind that here was Pastor Craig meeting with a well-known sinner at a bar. I felt like people were staring at us, thinking exactly that. But as I'd pre-decided to live my life for an audience of one, I reset my mind, remembering that Jesus was often criticized for "eating with the sinners" and that he says, "It is not the healthy who need a doctor, but the sick. I have not come to call the righteous, but sinners" (Mark 2:16–17).

So I sat with this guy, we had a great conversation, and I could see him making spiritual progress, moving closer to faith in Jesus.

How cool is that? *That's* our mission!

But by the time I returned to my office, we'd already had two phone calls from members of other churches who felt obligated to let someone know that Pastor Craig Groeschel was sitting—in a bar!—with a sinner! What they should have called to say was "We just saw your pastor acting like Jesus!"

For some reason, it's easy for us as Christians to lose our identity and turn inward. But as Sadie said, we are influencers. We know it. So we go—to be salt and light, to influence people whom God loves and who need Jesus. (Even if that means risking ridicule for being seen in a bar.) We will pre-decide:

I will be an influencer.

But it won't be easy. So we're going to pre-decide to influence others with our

1. prayers,
2. example, and
3. words.

I Will Influence with My Prayers

As we lose our identity and turn inward, we tend to pray benign, safe, small prayers.

- "God bless Grandma Ethel."
- "Lord, give me a good day."
- "Keep me safe as I make the one-mile drive to the grocery store."

Then there's the ever-popular "nourish our bodies" prayer. You know, "Dear Lord God, I pray you will bless this food to the nourishment of our bodies." A bad prayer? No. But when you're praying it over a greasy double bacon cheeseburger and chili fries? Or over fried Twinkies at the state fair? You're praying for *that* to nourish your body? Sorry if it offends, but that takes more faith than praying for God to part the Red Sea.

I believe we can and should pray about everything, but maybe we should pray some bigger prayers. I want to encourage you to make your prayers a strategic part of your influence.

We want to influence those who are far from Jesus to come close to him. God loves those people, and he wants them to come to him even more than we do. We have no greater power than God's, so we want to invite him to empower us.

We need to pray for our friends who are far from Jesus, and we need to pray for ourselves that we'll be ready to make the most of every opportunity.

That's what Paul counsels: "Devote yourselves to prayer, being watchful and thankful. And pray for us, too, that God may open a door for our message, so that we may proclaim the mystery of Christ, for which I am in chains. Pray that I may proclaim it clearly, as I should.

Be wise in the way you act toward outsiders; make the most of every opportunity. Let your conversation be always full of grace, seasoned with salt, so that you may know how to answer everyone" (Col. 4:2–6).

Paul's prayer is powerful. Notice he says we should *devote* ourselves to prayer. (Remember, we've pre-decided that we will be devoted.) He doesn't say, "Hey, you might want to maybe remember to pray about this if it comes to mind." No, he instructs us to pre-decide to pray consistently. Pray for what? As Paul advises, ask that you will

- be watchful for open doors to proclaim Christ;
- be wise in the way you act toward those who are outside the faith; and
- make the most of every opportunity to share Jesus, being always ready to give graceful answers to everyone.

Here is what Paul is urging us to do:

> Talk *to* God about people who are far from him.
> Talk *about* God with people who are far from him.

You might want to reread those two sentences carefully and think about how they work together.

This leads us to three ways we can have influence with our prayers:

1. Pray that God will give you open doors to share Christ with people who are far from him.
2. Pray that others who are close to God will share Christ with people who are far from him.
3. Pray that people who are far from God will receive the message of Christ and walk through those open doors.

Pray for Yourself

When you pray for yourself, what do you pray for?

Maybe a raise? Some time off work? Your kid to behave? Lower gas prices? Abs? (They've got to be under there somewhere!)

Do you pray that God will open doors for you to share Christ with people who are far from him? That God will give you eyes to see and words to speak when those opportunities arise?

Living that way would give your life purpose and meaning as you join Jesus in his mission. You would truly be an influencer and leave a legacy of changed lives when your life on earth is over.

If that's true, and it *is*, then we need to pray for open doors.

> When we pray for open doors, God will open some.

I have shared many times how, for more than twenty years, several days a week I met my buddy Paco at the gym and we'd work out together. One day we had a miscommunication, and he didn't show up. I was a little annoyed but had to, you know, exercise grace. So I worked out by myself and then headed into the sauna. I always go in there because you get really sweaty and then when you walk through the gym, people think, *Wow, you had a hard workout!* And I just give them a look, like *Yeah, hard workouts are my deal.*

So I was sitting in the sauna by my lonesome for the first time in twenty years when this guy walked in. He didn't say a word, but his body language was speaking volumes. I could tell something was bothering him. I said, "Hey. It seems obvious you're having a rough day. I don't want to pry, but if you want to talk, I'll listen." He hemmed and hawed for a few moments, probably deciding whether he should talk to a total stranger.

As he paused, I prayed a silent prayer.

Then he opened up.

He didn't go into all of the details, but he confided that he'd cheated on his wife and they got into a big fight. Assuming his marriage was over, he left home the day before. He broke down as he told me, "I'll never forget my three-year-old daughter, as my car backed out of the driveway, yelling, 'Daddy, don't leave us, don't leave us!' But I just drove down the street."

In that moment I realized that Paco's not showing up was not a mistake. I pray for open doors to share the message of Christ with people who are far from God, and he had given me one.

I said, in the most normal, nonpastor way I could, "Dude . . . I don't want to sound overly religious and I don't know where you stand with God, but I believe he wants you to know that your marriage doesn't have to be over."

He looked up at me through his tears, as if he desperately wanted to believe there still might be hope to keep his family together.

Feeling led by the Spirit, I let my words flow as if they weren't my own. "I believe God wants you to be daddy to your little girl and a faithful husband to your wife. What if," I asked him gently, "you drove home, got down on your knees, apologized sincerely, and asked your wife to forgive you?"

The guy fell apart. He said, "I'm not a religious guy or a church guy, but I think God sent you here to tell me that today."

So. Cool.

Influence.

Why?

Because I prayed for it. I prayed God would give me an open door to share the message of Christ with someone far from him. The "mistake" of Paco not showing up that day left me wide open to the opportunity of noticing my new friend.

The guy left the gym. He got down on his knees. He repented of his sin. Last I heard, his marriage is better than it's ever been, and they rarely miss church to give glory to the God who saved their family.

Do you pray for those God-prompted moments? He made you to make a difference and love people who don't yet believe. If you pray for it, God will give you opportunities to share the love and hope of Jesus. It may feel intimidating, but you can do this because he will help you and because you are an influencer.

Pray for People Who Are Close to God

In my early days after I had come to Christ, the first time I heard someone talk about the book of Philemon, I thought it was filet mignon. Nope.

Philemon is a little book in the New Testament. (How little? No chapters, just verses.) It's a personal letter Paul wrote to his friend Philemon, who seems to have been a successful businessman and hosted a small house church. Philemon owned some slaves, which was a common practice at the time and was typically based on personal indebtedness, not race. One of his slaves, Onesimus, ran away, all the way to Rome.

After he arrived, Onesimus met Paul. Paul led this slave into a relationship with Jesus. He was radically transformed, and he decided, "I need to go back to Philemon and make things right."

Paul penned a heartfelt letter to Philemon, vouching for Onesimus. He urged Philemon to receive Onesimus as a brother in the Lord, which he now was. Paul wrote, "I always thank my God as I remember you in my prayers, because I hear about your faith in the Lord Jesus and your love for all the saints" (Philem. vv. 4–5 NIV 1984). Paul thanked God for how Philemon loved other Christians.

Then he wrote, "I pray that you may be active in sharing your faith, so that you will have a full understanding of every good thing we have in Christ" (Philem. v. 6 NIV 1984).

Paul wanted Philemon to fully understand all of the blessings we have in Jesus. How does that happen?

By actively sharing our faith.

Do you want the people you love to have a full understanding of every good thing they have in Christ? Sure! We all do! Then we should pray for them that they would continually be active in sharing their faith.

I have a theory. It's not documented. But applying the context, here it is:

Remember, Philemon's slave ran away to Rome, where he met Paul. Onesimus was probably hurting. He was spiritually lost. Paul hit it off with him. Paul shared his story of how he met the risen Christ and it changed him. He told Onesimus, "You need to know Jesus." Onesimus said yes. He was transformed.

Paul was getting to know him more and asked, "Where did you come from?" Onesimus answered, "I work for a guy named Philemon." Paul said, "Philemon? Dude, I know him! He's amazing. He has a church that meets in his house! And wait. Wait. You worked for Philemon? And you're not a follower of Jesus? Didn't Philemon tell you about Jesus? No? He didn't?"

And so Paul told Philemon, "I love your love for all the saints. Like, bro, you're great at loving Christians." But he wrote, "I pray that you may be active in sharing your faith." Don't forget our mission!

We've been called to go.

To be salt and light.

To season.

To shine.

To share Jesus.

I think Paul knew that it's dangerously easy for Christians to move into an inward-looking, self-centered version of Christianity. We love our brothers and sisters in Christ, but rather than also loving those who are far from God, we might be judgmental or apathetic toward them. Instead of reaching out, we're retreating. Instead of joining the conversation, we're judging the conduct.

That's unacceptable, and that's why Paul prays that we would continually share our faith in Jesus. That's when we embrace our identity as influencers, having an impact on the lives of others. But something else happens. Paul says by sharing your faith you get a full understanding of every good thing you have in Christ.

At the end of his legendary "armor of God" passage in Ephesians 6, Paul closes by saying, "Pray also for me, that whenever I speak, words may be given me so that I will fearlessly make known the mystery of the gospel.... Pray that I may declare it fearlessly, as I should" (vv. 19–20). Notice Paul asks twice to be fearless in sharing his faith.

It's so easy for Christians to turn inward and become insular, and that's why we need to pray that others who are close to God will share the message of Christ with people who are far from God.

And pray that God will give you open doors to share Christ with people who are far from God.

And pray that people who are far from God will receive the message of Christ and walk through those open doors.

Pray for People Who Are Far from God

If you want to effect change in people's lives by pointing them to Jesus, start by praying for them. Pre-decide to pray for people who are far from God.

What do you pray for them?

- Pray that God would open their hearts. Lydia came to faith because "the Lord opened her heart to pay attention to what was said by Paul" (Acts 16:14 ESV).
- Pray that God would give them spiritual sight to understand and accept the gospel. We ask God to "open their eyes, so they may turn from darkness to light and from the power of Satan to God" (Acts 26:18 NLT).
- Pray that God would lead them to repentance. "God may perhaps grant them repentance leading to a knowledge of the truth, and they may come to their senses and escape from the snare of the devil" (2 Tim. 2:25–26 ESV).
- Pray that God would give you the words to say to them. To repeat Paul's plea, "Pray also for me, that whenever I speak, words may be given me so that I will fearlessly make known the mystery of the gospel" (Eph. 6:19).

Do you know a few people who are far from God? Do you pray for them daily? That connection is powerful. It's part of how I came to faith.

There was a movie back in the '80s called *Revenge of the Nerds*, but I want to tell you about the Prayer of the Nerds. After I became a Christian in college, three guys came up to me with scientific calculators snugly in their pocket protectors. They introduced themselves and told me they had gone to a big party the first weekend of the first year of college, back when we were all freshmen. They said I was the drunkest, most obnoxious guy at the party. That night they decided to make me their prayer project and had prayed for me every single day since. Now that I had become a Christian, they just wanted to say hi.

Wow.

Why did I come to faith? I think I should give credit to the Godly Geek Squad (who also became close friends of mine).

Their prayers changed my life.

You can influence others with your prayers.

Do you know a few people who are far from God for whom you could pray daily?

Pre-decide to pray for them.

I Will Influence with My Example

When you know who you are, you'll know what to do.

Right?

If you're Superman, and Lois Lane is in danger, no one has to tell you, "Now is the time to go into the phone booth and remove your suit and glasses, then burst out in your spandex and fly to her—you do remember you can fly, right?—and rescue her." No, Superman knows to do all of that 'cause he's Superman.

An example that's closer to home: Because I am a pastor, people always ask me to pray whenever there's a time to pray. "We're going to eat? Craig's here! Craig, will you pray?" "Someone is sick. Craig, you should pray." "Our football team's down by two points with one minute left? Craig's here! Craig, pray for a miracle comeback!" I'm not sure I should always be the one who's asked to pray, but I've never said, "Pray? Wait. What? Now?!"

I know who I am, so I know what to do.

I imagine if a plumber is at a party and someone comes screaming out of the bathroom, "The toilet is overflowing! The toilet is overflowing!" that plumber will burst into action. Why?

When you know who you are, you know what to do.

So who are you?

Remember Jesus says you are the salt of the earth and the light of the world.

That's who you are. You are salt. You are light.

When he said those words, people considered salt the second most important commodity on earth. The sun was number one, as it was the source of light. Salt was number two because of all it could do, especially in an age before refrigeration and other modern conveniences.

In ancient Rome people were often paid for their labor in salt. That's where we get our phrase "He's not worth his salt."

Jesus says, "You are salt."

What does salt do?

First, salt preserves. It keeps meat from rotting. As Christians we should have a preserving influence in the world. We represent the kingdom of God and his holiness by our good, pure lives.

Second, salt heals. Maybe you've had a sore in your mouth and gargled with salt water so it would get better. Salt speeds up the healing process. In the same way, God sends us to bring healing to people who have been wounded in life or hurt by religion.

Third, salt creates thirst. Bars often serve free peanuts or pretzels because their salt makes you thirsty, and so, in theory, you'll order more to drink, which will drive up your tab. Dasani bottled water contains salt. Sure, it's a mineral, but it also makes you want more water. Salt creates thirst. As a Christian, when you're full of God's love, you will create a divine thirst in other people. They'll ask, "What is it about you? Why are you so full of joy? I want what you have!" Salt creates thirst. Jesus says, "You are salt."

He also says, "You are the light of the world. A town built on a hill cannot be hidden. Neither do people light a lamp and put it under a bowl. Instead they put it on its stand, and it gives light to everyone in the house. In the same way, let your light shine before others, that they may see your good deeds and glorify your Father in heaven" (Matt. 5:14–16).

Jesus said those words long before the discovery of electricity. At night it would be pitch dark, so they would light a candle. Without lighters or matches, this was not easy. If the family left the house, they would place a bowl upside down over the candle to protect it from going out while they were away. A little hole in the bottom of the bowl would allow the fire to breathe so it would keep burning. But you'd never put the bowl on top of a candle when you were in the house. You need the light!

Jesus was telling his followers, who would always live in a dark world, never to cover their light. He was helping them understand they could live a life others want.

As light, you are an influencer.

God wants you to effect change in people as you point them to Jesus.

That happens as you are salt and light. The world needs salt because it is impure. The world needs light because it is dark.

Because you are a light, you don't run from the darkness, you shine in it. Remember, darkness exists only in the absence of light. When it's bedtime, no one says, "Would you mind turning on the darkness?" No, we say, "Please turn off the light."

Because you are salt, you don't run from the impurities, you cleanse them, and God uses you as an agent of change as you set an example of purity, which creates thirst in others.

Sometimes Christians will say, "I don't feel like salt. And I don't feel like light." I get that, but it doesn't matter. Because if you follow Jesus, you *are* salt and you *are* light.

They might respond, "Well, I guess maybe if I learn the Bible better, I'd be able to answer people's questions . . ."

No. Most people don't care how much you know. They just want to know how much you care.

Jesus made that point in the parable of the Good Samaritan, as the priest and the Levite ignored and avoided the injured man. The "regular guy," the man the priest and Levite would have looked down on, was the only one who cared enough to stop and help (Luke 10:25–37).

You are salt. You are light. And when you know who you are, you'll know what to do. How you love, how you care for people, flows out of who you are.

It's time to be salt and to shine your light. When you do, people will notice. They will "see your good deeds and glorify your Father in heaven" (Matt. 5:16).

People Will Notice

Paul and Silas were two early followers of Jesus. When they gave their lives to Christ, he radically transformed them. They knew they were salt and light, and when you know who you are, you know what to do.

Everywhere they went, they were telling people about Jesus. The religious authorities didn't like that and told them to stop. But they would not stop. How could they? They were salt and light.

The authorities arrested and beat them, but they kept telling everyone what Jesus had done in their lives. In Acts 16 we see the authorities arrest them and have them stripped, beaten with rods, flogged, and imprisoned (Acts 16:22–24).

Read that last sentence again, then pause for a second.

They were stripped naked in public.

They were beaten with rods.

They were flogged, which likely means they were whipped thirty-nine times across the back with a whip that would have little pieces of glass and rocks embedded in it. It was designed to rip your body open until your internal organs were exposed and bring you to the point of death, or to the point of wishing for death, without actually killing you.

Then they were put in a dungeon and their legs put in stocks. To increase the torture, the jailer would take the prisoner's legs and spread them out as far as possible before clamping them down.

We've all had bad days. Like when you tried to scale the outside of a historic church building, came face-to-face with a potentially rabid bobcat, or your wife gave you "that look" at a party when you were killing it with your comedy.

But Paul and Silas had more than just a bad day. So how did they respond to being tortured and imprisoned for talking about Jesus? "About midnight Paul and Silas were praying and singing hymns to God, and the other prisoners were listening to them" (Acts 16:25).

What were they doing? Being salt and light.

They were being who they were.

They didn't have an emergency meeting where Paul said, "Okay, we've had a really bad day. Now here we are and look who else is here. Other prisoners. And we're supposed to be Christians. So I guess we better represent. What do you think we should do?"

No. They didn't think about what to do. They were praying and praising God because it was who they were. They were salt and light. They were influencers.

When you are salt and light, people will notice.

I think of when a staff member's husband had a massive heart attack. He was only thirty-eight years old. For more than ninety minutes he had no heartbeat. The paramedics kept him alive manually by repeatedly pounding on his chest and shocking him back to life. When I got to the hospital, I learned that it was unlikely he'd survive, and if he did, he would be brain dead.

Hundreds of people from our church showed up over the next several days and we prayed and worshiped. We weren't trying to be good witnesses, we were just being who we were, salt and light, and people noticed.

Members of the hospital staff wrote about it online, saying they had never seen anything like it. One nurse, a guy named Dan, came back in on his day off just to be around and try to figure out what was going on. He finally asked, "You all must be church people, right?" When we said yes, he asked, "What church do you go to?" We told him, and he asked, "Can I come? I've just never seen anything like this. I mean, well, can I come?" And he did!

You know who else was at our church service the following week? The heart attack victim, alive, with no brain damage.

It was a miracle.

The same thing happened in Paul and Silas's prison cell. They were singing praises and then a violent earthquake hit, opening the prison doors and shaking the chains off their legs (Acts 16:26).

God showed up and showed off.

We're told that "the jailer woke up"—whoops, sleeping on the job, Mr. Jailer? "The jailer woke up, and when he saw the prison doors open, he drew his sword and was about to kill himself because he thought the prisoners had escaped" (Acts 16:27).

He knew if the prisoners escaped, he would be executed. He must have thought, "I'd rather do it myself and spare the public humiliation."

"But Paul shouted, 'Don't harm yourself! We are all here!'" (Acts 16:28).

Paul and Silas had a chance to escape but chose not to leave.

That's amazing!

The prison cell felt like where God was not. It was darkness.

So many Christians today want to run from the darkness. They see people who listen to mainstream music and drink and have tattoos and watch *Game of Thrones* and they want to run from all of it.

Darkness is not something you run from. You are light, so you shine into it. That's what light does.

Paul and Silas didn't leave, because they knew who they were. As an incredible act of love, they stayed in the darkness and gave the jailer hope.

That's why we pre-decide, "I will influence with my example and see the darkness as an opportunity to shine."

After my senior year of college, I felt called into ministry, but no one was calling. So I took the only job I could get, selling home security systems. I was excited because I was coming out of a wild college environment and thought there would be less temptation in a real-world job. I was wrong. The people who worked at my new company made my fraternity brothers seem like a bunch of Boy Scouts.

On my first day some coworkers asked, "Want to go to lunch with us?" I was excited to be invited. "Sure! Where are we going?" They said, "To the strip club!" I thought, *No. I'm not going to compromise on my first day on the job.*

So I lied. I couldn't think of what else to do. I said, "Oh, um, oh yeah, I forgot, I . . . brought something. I've got a sandwich in my lunch box in the car."

Really? I've got a sandwich in a lunch box in a car? Fortunately, they didn't ask questions. "What kind of lunch box you got, bro? SpongeBob SquarePants?" "Why did you leave a sandwich in a hot car? You that dumb?"

Later that day the girl at the front desk smiled and joked with me. "Don't wear Polo cologne. 'Cause if a guy wears Polo, I get with that guy." Huh? She laughed and told me she'd been hurt by too many men and "wanted to conquer every man she could."

Then another new coworker shared with me how she'd been hurt in a relationship and was trying to figure her way out of the pain.

I also got to meet an installer, a good ol' boy who seemed as disinterested in God as a person could get.

I went home after that first day and told Amy, "They want to take me to a strip club! And . . . Polo cologne! And you should hear the things these people say! I can't work there. It's just too dark!"

Amy looked me in the eyes and asked, "Craig, don't you think God sent you there to make a difference?"

I was like, "Oh yeah, I forgot about that."

Amy was asking me to break free from my disappointment in the moment and think ahead to the impact I could make on these people for Jesus.

And I decided, I *pre*-decided, that I would influence those people with my prayers, my example, and my words.

Amy and I started praying like crazy for all of these people and loving them in every way we could. We knew salt works only if there's contact with food, and light has impact only when it comes into contact with darkness. So we committed to spend time with them and grow our relationships. We went to their parties. We would drink water as they got sloshed. We had them to our house for dinner. We got to know their spouses and children.

That's what we do.

We are salt and light, and when we live that out, people will notice.

They'll notice, and people will be changed.

People Will Be Changed

Once the prison guard realized they were still there, he "rushed in and fell trembling before Paul and Silas" (Acts 16:29). He had witnessed their faith and experienced their love, so he asked, "Sirs, what must I do to be saved?" (Acts 16:30).

He had heard them preaching when they were told to stop and worhiping when they shouldn't have been. He had seen God work, and it had created a thirst in him.

He wanted what they had.

They told him, "Believe in the Lord Jesus, and you will be saved—you and your household" (Acts 16:31), and that is exactly what happened. The jailer and his family were baptized that night, and their lives were changed.

That's what happens when we stay in the darkness and shine Jesus' light.

That's what happened at my job too. I worked there for only ten months before going into full-time ministry, but Amy and I were able to lead about a third of my coworkers to Christ.

The front-desk Polo girl gave her life to Christ and joined the church I was a part of at the time. She had a beautiful voice and sang in the choir, staying at that church years after I left, until she moved to another city.

The other coworker put her faith in Jesus and was a part of our church in the early years until she died of cancer.

I lost track of my favorite installer until I was visiting our South Oklahoma City church. After the service someone came up and said, "Pastor Craig, I love you! I love our church!" I looked up and was like, "No way! What are you doing here?"

All of that happened as the result of ten short months of my being salt and light. And none of that was done by Pastor Craig. It was all Security-Alarm-Selling Craig. All because, no matter the location or the vocation, I knew who I was.

Salt and light.

And when you know who you are, you know what to do.

I Will Influence with My Words

One day at the gym, I noticed this guy. I noticed him because he was huge. His muscles had muscles, which had muscles. Although he looked confident on the outside, I could tell he was troubled on the inside. Seeing him consistently, I started to care for and pray for my new friend.

One day he came up to me and said, "I want what you have."

I was looking at his muscles (well, more accurately, at his muscles' muscles) and thought, *No, I want what you have.*

He continued. "I'm serious. There's something different about you. I want what you have."

Why did that happen?

Because I had pre-decided to influence him with my prayers and my example. That gave me the opportunity to influence him with my words, and that's when it gets fun!

That reminds me of when Jesus approached a Samaritan woman at a well.

The conversation they were about to have should never have happened. Back then, Jews did not travel into Samaria. The Samaritans were half Jewish, half gentile, and the Jews hated them. Jews did not interact with Samaritans.

Also, men did not interact with women. And this was not just any woman. Let's just say that no one was impressed with her example. She had gone from man to man to man. She traveled to the well at noon, when it was hottest and no one else would be there, to avoid the stares of people who judged her for her lifestyle.

Jesus once said, "I am the light of the world. Whoever follows me will never walk in darkness, but will have the light of life" (John 8:12), and he was about to shine his light into her darkness. He said he came to proclaim the good news (Luke 4:18), and he was about to share it with her. Let's see how Jesus influenced her with his words, because, as always, we can learn a lot from him.

Start with the Superficial

Jesus first asked her, "Will you give me a drink?" (John 4:7). Notice he started the conversation on a superficial level based on their immediate circumstances.

He didn't start with "I am the Messiah, sent by God—now repent of your sins." Some Christians who have spiritual conversations jump in faster and furiouser than Vin Diesel in a street-racing movie. You might want to slow down, Speedy Gonzales.

On the other hand, some Christians hesitate from having spiritual conversations because they don't know how to initiate one. Start on a superficial level based on your immediate situation. You know, small talk. Talk about your job to your coworker, about your neighborhood to your neighbor, about the game to your sports-fan friend. Get the conversation going with whatever feels natural. That allows God to open the spiritual door.

From Superficial to Spiritual

Soon Jesus told her, "Everyone who drinks this water will be thirsty again, but whoever drinks the water I give them will never thirst. Indeed, the water I give them will become in them a spring of water welling up to eternal life" (John 4:13–14).

Jesus transitioned from superficial to spiritual, and at some point we need to do the same in our conversations with people who are far from God. I like how Jesus used something important from her everyday life to reveal her need for God. We can do that too.

Jesus gave her the opportunity to talk, to share her opinions and ask questions. She talked as much as Jesus did. Unfortunately, today, some Christians can have a reputation for talking and talking but never listening. We need to follow Jesus' example and have gracious dialogues with people instead of giving monologues.

From Spiritual to Personal

This woman noticed something different about this man, so she asked, "Sir, give me this water so that I won't get thirsty and have to keep coming here to draw water" (John 4:15).

Jesus responded, "Go and get your husband" (John 4:16 TLB).

She told him she didn't have a husband, and Jesus said to her, "You are right when you say you have no husband. The fact is, you have had five husbands, and the man you now have is not your husband. What you have just said is quite true" (John 4:17–18).

She just learned that the one who matters most knew everything about what she had done but was still dignifying her with his respect.

He didn't treat her as an immoral woman but as a miracle waiting to happen. We can do the same with the people God puts in our path. We take the conversation from superficial to spiritual to personal.

When we talk about personal things, about the person's need for Jesus, we do it in the most respectful, gracious way possible.

I love how Jesus used his words to influence her. And I love how she—someone who might have been voted least likely to be an influencer in the entire New Testament—then used her words to influence others: "Then, leaving her water jar, the woman went back to the town and said to the people, 'Come, see a man who told me everything I ever did. Could this be the Messiah?' They came out of the town and made their way toward him" (John 4:28–30).

She used her words to remind people of her story—a story she had been ashamed of only an hour or so earlier. And we get to share our stories and how we were changed when we met Jesus.

She also used her words to invite people to meet Jesus, and it's powerful when we invite our coworkers, neighbors, and friends to come to a church service or small group where they have a chance to encounter Jesus.

We learn from this woman that you don't need to have it all together to influence someone for Jesus. She had a salacious background and didn't know any Bible verses. She wasn't even totally convinced about Jesus yet! Notice she asked the townspeople, "Could this be the Messiah?" But if you keep reading, you discover that a revival breaks out as many Samaritans come to faith in Jesus.

Who did God use to influence a whole city? Not an Instagram star, or a professional athlete, or a celebrity, or a pastor.

God used an ordinary, broken, sinful woman who had been transformed by Jesus.

You are an influencer and God wants to use you.

He can use your prayers, your example, and your words.

When Dwayne Johnson's long-lost twin brother came up to me in the gym and said, "I want what you have," I told him, in normal, nonreligious language, "What's special about me, what I have, is not self-discipline. It's not positive thinking. It's Jesus. Jesus is what I have. And you can have him too."

If you let your light shine, people will be attracted to the light. They will want what you have. And you can share your greatest treasure. You can help them know the unconditional love of God displayed through his sinless son, Jesus.

4.5

The Long Game

Back in college there was a great athlete who I respected. We were in different friend groups and didn't know each other well. But we were often at parties together and always had good interactions.

When I became a Christian, it was big news at our little school because, as I've mentioned, I was known as a wild partier. One day this guy came up to me and asked, "What's up with this religious stuff? You were fun before!"

I laughed. "I know. I know."

He was confused. "I just don't understand."

"I don't expect you to understand," I told him. "I wouldn't have understood it before either. But here's the deal. One day, when you're ready to talk about spiritual things, I want you to call me. I don't care when it is, call me. I want to be the one to talk to you about it!"

He insisted, "Well, I will make a promise to you. That will never happen."

Not exactly the conversation I'd hoped to have.

If you've tried to share Jesus with people, you've probably had a few times when you were rejected and walked away dejected.

What do you do?

Commit to the long game.

I have found that salt and light often work best over time.

Knowing how patient and persistent God has been with us, we need to show that same patience and persistence to the people God loves. We need to love people enough to stay committed to the long game.

Decades to Make a Difference

My not-so-close friend and I both graduated and moved on. More than two decades went by, and then one day I ran into him. I could tell from his countenance that he was in a very rough season.

I said, "You're ready to talk, aren't you?"

He sounded a bit embarrassed as he told me, "Yeah, I am."

After a long silence, he told me the details of his personal heartbreaks and tragic losses. This strong, athletic guy I hardly knew broke down crying. Not knowing what to say, I gave him an awkward hug, trying my best to show him that I cared.

Finally he managed to pull himself together and said, "Okay, I'll go to your stupid church."

I laughed. "I didn't invite you to my stupid church."

"I know," he said, "but you were going to, weren't you?"

"I was!"

He said, "I'll go!"

He and his thirteen-year-old daughter came that Sunday, and she gave her life to Christ. He called me a few days later and said, "I don't get it, but the same thing that happened to you happened to her. Craig, it's probably going to happen to me, isn't it?"

I told him, "Yes, it is!"

He said, "Well, then, let's get together and get it over with!"

We got together and he prayed a life-transforming prayer, putting his faith in Jesus and committing to follow him forever.

It was a lot like what happened with Paul and Silas's jailer, except there was no earthquake, and instead of a few hours, it took more than twenty years!

More. Than. Twenty. Years.

Committed to the long game, I never gave up on him, because God loves him and because God has never given up on me.

Maybe you're tempted to give up on someone. Don't stop praying. Don't stop believing. And don't give up. You are salt and light. You run into the darkness, and you shine the love of Jesus into it. God made you to make a difference and you need to be who you are. You are an influencer.

So pre-decide: I am an influencer.

PART 4 EXERCISES

1. List areas of your life where you connect with and may influence other people. Think of daily, weekly, and monthly interactions to cover everywhere possible.
2. Do you tend to be someone who "eats with sinners" or to be the one who criticizes those who do? Why do you make that choice?
3. Why do you think so many Christians eventually lose their identity and turn inward when it comes to expressing and sharing their faith?
4. Have you ever led someone to Christ? Write down what happened.
5. Here's a three-part question:
   - Write down the name of one person you know who is far from God right now.
   - How can you pray for that person to come to know Jesus? Be specific.
   - How can you talk about God with that person? Be specific.
6. Write a prayer asking God to give you open doors to share him, eyes to see those opportunities, and words to say when those moments come. Consider making this an ongoing prayer.
7. Are you the only light within your circles of influence, like me at my first job? What steps can you take to shine brighter and be a stronger influence for Christ?
8. Within your circles of influence, is there someone showing interest in spiritual things with whom you simply need to engage? Plan how you can take the next steps with that person.
9. Is there a relationship in your life in which you need to commit to the long game? Do you need to reengage with or recommit to praying for someone?

I Will Be Generous

*But generous people plan to do
what is generous,
and they stand firm in their
generosity.*

—ISAIAH 32:8 NLT

5.1

How to Be More Blessed

On an airplane, do you prefer the window or aisle seat?

If window, guess what? You are more selfish than other people. Sound dumb? I agree, but I'm biased because I prefer the window seat too. But it's the conclusion social scientists came to after studying who opts for which seats.[18]

If you're feeling a little defensive right now, that might be a sign that you are selfish. But don't worry, it also turns out people raised in church tend to be more selfish.[19] Those who have lower emotional intelligence are also more selfish,[20] as are those who go to the gym,[21] take more time to make decisions,[22] study economics,[23] or are rich.[24] There is research that tells us men are more selfish.[25] But before you celebrate, ladies, there is other research suggesting that it is actually women who are more selfish—especially when it comes to chocolate.[26]

So what's the conclusion?

We are all selfish.

All of us except women who choose the middle seat on a flight, were not raised in church, never work out, make rash decisions, are poor, have an aversion to studying economics, and don't like chocolate. Population of that group? Eight. Yes, I did some research myself, and there are eight people in the world who fit that description.

The rest of us?

Selfish.

We are all naturally selfish.

You may be thinking, "Not me. I really care about people. I'm a giver. Just ask my mom. She'll tell you I'm the best!"

You might want to slow down before giving yourself the Mother

Teresa Most Selfless Person on the Planet Award. Because as it turns out, you're not as selfless as you think.

We are all selfish, but no one thinks they're selfish.

We're hardwired not to detect selfishness in ourselves. That's been proven too.[27] Dr. Molly Crockett, associate professor at Princeton University, explains that the research shows "when people behave in ways that fall short of their personal standards, one way they maintain their moral self-image is by misremembering their ethical lapses."

Huh?

She's saying you lie to yourself! You lie to yourself to maintain your cherished self-image of not being selfish. As the Creator, God revealed this to us thousands of years before social scientists were able to prove it: "The heart is deceitful above all things and beyond cure" (Jer. 17:9).

We're naturally selfish. But it gets worse—something stokes our selfishness thousands of times a day.

I read an article written in 2007, before Instagram. Before Netflix originals. Before Cash App. Before we'd heard of avocado toast. How did we live?! Back in 2007 the average person on an average day was exposed to about five thousand advertisements! Perhaps not your weird cousin who lives off the grid in a shack in the woods. But unless you are that weird cousin (and, if so, how did you hear about this book?), you were exposed to five thousand ads a day, every day.

Crazy, right?

The world has changed. We have social media, influencers, games on our phones, and avocado toast available at many hip restaurants. Now how many ads do we see a day?

About ten thousand!

Uh-oh. That is not good news for us.

Why? Studies show that the more ads we see, the more miserable we are. All of those ads remind us of what we don't have but think we need to be happy. (Commercials should start with a disclaimer: "And now, thirty seconds to make you miserable!") We are told ten thousand times a day that you cannot have the good life without the new iPhone, car, sneakers, or Lululemon leggings. The ads insist, "You need to get to be happy. Get what? Get that, and that, and that, and that. Get more."

We're conditioned to believe our lives will be incomplete until we acquire and accumulate more.

Our culture tells us it is more blessed to get.

Jesus offers a countercultural message. He says, "It is more blessed to give than to receive" (Acts 20:35).

Did you get that?

> You will be blessed more when you give.

The word in the original Greek language translated "blessed" means happy. So if you want to be happy, give, don't get. Instead of being a slave to your instincts and purchasing what looks good in the moment, think ahead to the blessed life you want to live. You'll have more happiness when you become more generous.

What Jesus said two thousand years ago has been proven today. Studies have found the following:

- People who gave money to charity were 43 percent more likely than nongivers to say they were "very happy."
- Those who gave money were 34 percent less likely than nongivers to have felt "so sad that nothing could cheer them up" and were 68 percent less likely to have felt hopeless.
- People who gave their time volunteering were 42 percent more likely to be very happy than those who don't volunteer.[28]

These studies are telling us that if you want to be happy, if you don't want to feel sad and hopeless, give. Jesus was right, it really is more blessed to give than to receive.

Our culture will continue to try to brainwash us with the intoxicating lie that it's more blessed to consume. But we need to embrace the truth Jesus tells us: it's more blessed to give.

Pause long enough to think about what you feel when you give, and you'll understand why it's more blessed.

Compare getting and giving. It *is* fun to get something new. But it's more than fun to give. It's also spiritual. It's rewarding. It's fulfilling. It's blessed. I'm guessing you have a few emotional giving stories where God prompted you to sacrifice to give. When you did, you likely felt overcome with emotional fulfillment.

You were blessed to be a blessing.

That's how to be more blessed.

Living a life marked by intentional generosity is meaningful beyond monetary measure. You sense God's joy when he uses you to show his love to others. It's emotional to give. But chances are slim you have many emotional "consuming" stories.

- You might have been excited to upgrade your iPhone, but I bet you didn't feel overwhelmed with spiritual fulfillment.
- You may have experienced a momentary rush of excitement wearing a new outfit on a date, but I'm guessing you didn't feel overwhelmed with the presence and joy of the Lord when you swiped your credit card to make your purchase.
- You felt a buzz of adrenaline while driving off in the car you just bought, but I doubt it led you to worship God knowing he used your purchase to change someone else's life.

Why? Consuming or getting may be fun, but giving is emotional. Giving is blessed by God.

Impulsive behavior or negative emotions can fuel us to consume, but the endorphin rush quickly fades. Generosity creates a lasting effect that feels good every time you think about it.

You may have seen one of the amazing YouTube videos of the moment when a deaf child hears for the first time. (If you haven't, you should watch one. Just don't do it when anyone is around, unless you don't mind someone seeing you ugly cry.) It's hard to tell who is most moved during the miracle moment. I watched several so I could understand the depth of emotions.

I watched one of a little boy who has never heard a sound before. Not his mom saying "I love you." Not his dad singing a lullaby. Not the crashing sounds of an ocean. Not the beauty of music. The child has never heard anything.

Thanks to the miracle of modern medicine, a small device makes hearing possible. Sitting in the lap of his mom, he hears her softly say his name. For the first time ever, he hears.

The boy's eyes are wide. His mouth drops open. His hands are raised in excitement. He smiles the biggest smile of his entire life.

Then there's mom and dad looking on. For the first time, their child can hear their voices. They burst into loud tear-laughter. What's tear-laughter? That's when someone is laughing so loud and crying so hard you can't call it laughing or crying. It's both. It's joy immeasurable. It's exuberant gratitude. It's a miracle.

Here's a question: Who is the most blessed person in that room? If you've watched one of these videos, you might be hard-pressed to decide.

The child who just heard his mom's words for the first time—that's blessed, right?

But then there's the mom and the dad. Their prayers have been answered. Their child can hear. Again, that's blessed, right?

But there's one more person in the room—the audiologist, the doctor who sacrificed and studied for years to put herself through school. Without her dedication and skills, this miracle moment would not have happened.

Who is most blessed? The child is likely the most shocked. The parents most grateful. But I'm guessing it's the doctor who is most fulfilled and blessed. Why? Because God used her to change a family's life.

Jesus said it so clearly. It's more blessed to give than to receive.

And so we want to be givers, generous givers.

You may think you are generous, but you're not sure. In this chapter I'll try to help you figure that out.

Or you may realize you're not generous but want to be. I think that's where many are today.

- They want to be generous but feel like they can't.
- They want more blessing and may need to realize Jesus said it comes from giving, not receiving.
- They want to be generous and hope someday they will be.

That is a great sentiment, but there's a problem with it:

No one accidentally becomes generous.

Think about the people you know. I'm certain you've never met anyone who tithes by mistake. You've never been friends with someone who accidentally gives, beyond their tithe, to fund ministries and mission trips and to help those in need. You'll never hear a testimony of someone who says, "I have no idea how, but every year I give a higher percentage of my income than the year before."

No one accidentally becomes generous.

But generous is exactly what we want to be. We want to obey God, want to receive his blessing, want to make a difference and leave a legacy. We want to live out 2 Corinthians 9:6–8, 11 (NIV 1984):

Remember this: Whoever sows sparingly will also reap sparingly, and whoever sows generously will also reap generously. Each man should give what he has decided in his heart to give, not reluctantly or under compulsion, for God loves a cheerful giver. And God is able to make all grace abound to you, so that in all things at all times, having all that you need, you will abound in every good work. . . . You will be made rich in every way so that you can be generous on every occasion, and through us your generosity will result in thanksgiving to God.

We want that! We want to

- sow generously so we can reap generously,
- see God's grace abound to us,
- be made rich in every way, and
- be so generous people thank God for us.

We want to be generous but don't think we can.
Yes, you can. You can if you pre-decide.

Stop Holding Back

People who are not generous but want to be usually think, *When I have more, I'll give more. One day I'll be able to afford to be generous.*

Nope.

That's not how it works, for anyone.

Generosity is not about what you have or don't have. Generosity is about your heart.

You know this. You've seen poor people who are stingy and other poor people who give extravagantly and sacrificially. You also know of rich people who are changing the world with strategic, full-blown generosity, and rich people who aren't willing to give a dime.

Generosity is not about how much you have, it's about your heart.

If you're not generous now, you won't be generous later.

If you had more money, chances are high that you would not give more—you'd likely give less (according to Stacy Palmer, the editor of the *Chronicle of Philanthropy*) and have mo' problems (according to Biggie). We know that because of the research. Recently in America, people who made

- less than $25,000 per year gave away 7.7 percent of their income;
- between $25,000 and $50,000 gave away 4.6 percent;
- between $50,000 and $75,000 gave away 3.5 percent;
- between $75,000 and $100,000 gave 3 percent;

- between \$100,000 and \$200,000 gave 2.6 percent; and
- \$200,000 or more, even millions, gave 2.8 percent.

People think they would give more if they made more. They wouldn't. People who make more spend more. They find more and more expensive things to buy. Or they put even more money into savings and retirement. They don't give more when they make more because it was never about the amount they made. It was always about their hearts.

If you are not generous now, you will not be generous later.

Jesus tells a parable in Luke 12 about a rich man who has a big harvest. His problem: he doesn't have enough room to store all of his stuff. What do you do at that point? You realize you have enough, so you can give the excess away. Right? Wrong. The rich man does what he's always done. He says, "I know! I'll tear down my barns and build bigger ones. Then I'll have room enough to store all my wheat and other goods. And I'll sit back and say to myself, 'My friend, you have enough stored away for years to come. Now take it easy! Eat, drink, and be merry!'" (Luke 12:18–19 NLT).

Why does he do what he has always done? Because more money does not make you more generous. More money makes you more of what you already are. More money doesn't change who you are, it just reveals who you are.

> If you want to be generous when you have more, learn to be generous when you have less.

To be generous later you must be generous now.

You probably agree but still may feel like you don't know how or just can't. That's where the power of decision comes in.

We are going to pre-decide:

> I will be generous.

I worship a generous God. "For God so loved the world, he gave." I follow a generous Savior. He's so generous he gave his life for me. Because my identity is rooted in Jesus, I will be generous.

> Giving is not just what I do. Generous is who I am.

You *are* generous, so it's time to start acting that way. It's time to make two decisions every generous person makes.

Generous People Plan to Be Generous

The first decision:

> Generous people plan to be generous.

You might say, "But I thought generosity was randomly blessing people. You know, see a need, meet a need."

- You see the guy on the side of the road with a sign and give him some cash.
- You buy someone's groceries because you feel a prompting.
- You spontaneously pay for the person behind you in the drive-through.
- You go to a fundraiser and the speaker is inspiring, and there's a big thermometer, and he shouts, "We need to fill it up! No one likes a half-full thermometer!" So you start feeling sad. *That is a pathetic-looking thermometer.* And guilty. *How can I not give? I mean, that poor thermometer.* And you write a check.
- You are watching TV at night and that commercial comes on with the sad, starving dogs and the Sarah McLachlan song about angels, and you're like, "No. This can't be! We need to help those dogs! And what about the angels? Who's with me and Sarah?!" so you send some money.

Isn't that generosity?

No. That is not generosity, that's giving.

To be clear, giving is good. Giving honors God. Giving meets needs.

Giving blesses people. Yes, you want to give. But giving is not the same as generosity.

Generous people don't have to see a need. They don't have to be inspired or guilted. They are not reactive. They don't give only when they have something extra.

What do generous people do?

A Plan

Generous people have a plan. Scripture tells us, "But generous people plan to do what is generous, and they stand firm in their generosity" (Isa. 32:8 NLT).

Generous people plan out their generosity and stand firm.

Most people have a plan for their finances. Their plan, however, is not to give but to consume, to spend, to buy. We plan for our next big purchase or vacation. If there is something we really want, we'll even do research. Which is the best model? What has the best ratings? Is it worth the extra one hundred dollars to get the 5-star rating instead of the 4½-star rating? We research and plan when it comes to receiving.

For example, I got to work researching when I decided I needed a small trailer. My unstated goal was to learn every detail about every model of trailer. I studied all of the ratings and reviews and narrowed it down to four options.

Then I shifted to finding the best deal. Some in other states were cheaper, but I'd have to drive to pick them up, so I had to factor in travel expenses. The middle-range options seemed to be a good value. But I found a higher-end trailer at a deep discount. I debated for a few days and then called the owner, only to find out it had already sold.

Weeks later I finally purchased one locally. I hooked it up to my Honda Pilot and put it in reverse, immediately jackknifing the trailer into my vehicle and doing more damage to my small SUV than the value of the whole trailer I had just purchased. (Have I mentioned I can be colossally stupid?)

The point is we research and plan when it comes to receiving. Some of us more than others.

But people who know it's more blessed to give than to receive plan their generosity. They strategize their giving. They ask God these things:

- "How can I give more?"
- "Where can I make a bigger difference?"
- "Whom can I bless?"
- "How do I maximize what you have given me?"

It is not spontaneous or haphazard, or driven by emotion.

It is intentional and strategic, and driven by a desire to honor God and live the kind of life he blesses.

Generous people have a plan.

You might be thinking, *But I'm not a planner.*

I'd argue you already have a financial plan. It may not be written, but you have a plan. It may not be a good plan, but you do have a plan.

Here is a typical plan for most people today. We'll call most people "Bob."

God provides Bob with money (Bob gets paid), and Bob spends it. Actually, Bob probably spends more than it, which is why the average American household is $101,915 in debt.[29] If God gives Bob an increase—maybe a raise or tax return or extra income from his side hustle selling avocado toast (Bob is on trend)—Bob will spend that money too. It's his chance to finally buy that faster car or slow cooker or bigger big-screen TV or smaller stomach (lipo, anyone?).

Bob spends what he gets, or more than he gets, which creates a lack of financial margin, which is why Bob worries so much about money. Bob will hear about living a generous life but thinks, *I can't. My finances are already too tight.* And Bob's lack of giving leads to a lack of blessing.

Bob would tell you he doesn't have a financial plan, but he *does.* It's just not written down. Also, it's not very good.

Bob would complain that he has a money problem. But he doesn't. He has a spiritual problem. He is looking to things to give him fulfillment that can be found only in Jesus. He's trusting in money rather than putting his faith in God.

That's Bob, but I wonder: Does Bob sound anything like you? Do you live out that same cycle?

The problem goes deeper because by spending instead of giving you are investing your money (check that, *God's* money) in things that don't last. But Jesus says, "Do not store up for yourselves treasures on earth, where moths and vermin destroy, and where thieves break in and steal. But store up for yourselves treasures in heaven, where moths and vermin do not destroy, and where thieves do not break in and steal. For where your treasure is, there your heart will be also" (Matt. 6:19–21).

You are stuck in a cycle that leads to lack of margin, lots of worry, lack of impact on earth, and lack of treasure in heaven.

You may find it frustrating. If so, you might describe what you have as a money problem. But it's not. It's a spiritual problem.

It's time to break the cycle. How? You realize financial *is* spiritual and you choose, as someone who is devoted, to put God first.

Putting God first with your finances breaks the cycle.

Remember Jesus says, "But seek first the kingdom of God and his righteousness, and all these things will be provided for you" (Matt. 6:33 CSB). He did not say seek first the Apple TV+ subscription, or seek first the new quartz countertops, or seek first the latest Jordans, or seek first tickets for the game. No, we seek God first in every way, including with our money. We worship and honor God by pre-deciding to be generous, and we trust God to provide what we really need.

So what is a good generosity plan?

God gives us one that is powerful and life-changing: the tithe. We read in Malachi 3:10: "Bring the whole tithe into the storehouse, that there may be food in my house."

The Hebrew word translated "tithe" is *hamma'aser*. It means tenth, or 10 percent. Return to God 10 percent of what he blesses you with as a way of putting him first in your finances, as an act of worship and obedience.

You might be thinking, *Whoa. Give 10 percent of all of the money I bring in? There's no way I could live off 90 percent. I can barely make it with 100 percent!*

I get it. The first time I heard about giving 10 percent back to God, I thought, *Whaaa? There's just no way. I can't afford to do that. I would have to rearrange my life. I'd have to make some significant changes to prioritize God and put him first.* It seemed impossible.

A Promise

I think God could foresee our reaction and our objections because this is the only time in Scripture when he tells us we can put him to the test. Everywhere else we are told not to test God, but here God encourages us to test him if we're hesitant or have doubts. "'Bring the whole tithe into the storehouse, that there may be food in my house. Test me in this,' says the LORD Almighty, 'and see if I will not throw open the floodgates of heaven and pour out so much blessing that there will not be room enough to store it'" (Mal. 3:10).

God promises he will provide for us if we put him first.

Some say the tithe is only an Old Testament principle. But five hundred years later Jesus affirmed the tithe and backed up God's guarantee with another promise to pour out blessing on those who tithe.

The Pharisees were being hypocritical (surprise, surprise), and Jesus told them they *should* tithe, but that they also needed to do justice, show mercy, and live by faith. While he was correcting them for their lack of love, he said, "You should tithe, yes, but do not neglect the more important things" (Matt. 23:23 NLT).

Jesus affirmed the tithe. He also confirmed God's promise to bless those who give generously: "Give, and it will be given to you. A good measure, pressed down, shaken together and running over, will be poured into your lap. For with the measure you use, it will be measured to you" (Luke 6:38).

Wow! I want that! Don't you want to get in on God's generosity plan?

The Priority

His plan is for us to give back to him 10 percent, the *first* 10 percent. We are told in Proverbs 3:9–10, "Honor the LORD with your wealth, with the firstfruits of all your crops; then your barns will be filled to overflowing, and your vats will brim over with new wine."

Did you notice it says *first*fruits? Generous people put God first. That takes faith. It doesn't take faith to give God your leftovers. *The offering is coming around. Let's see what I've got in my wallet. Oh, I've got twenty dollars. Yeah, I can toss that in.* That's not generosity, because it's not planned and it doesn't require faith. What takes faith is to give God the first 10 percent. "The purpose of tithing is to teach you always to put God first in your lives" (Deut. 14:23 TLB).

How do we give him the first 10 percent, use our faith, and make sure it's not leftovers? When you get paid, the tithe is the first financial transaction you make, not the last. If we wait until last, we will look at how much is left, and 10 percent quickly becomes 5 percent, or 3 percent, or 1 percent, or none. That's why giving to God first is such a crucial part of your decision to be generous.

And did you notice, in Proverbs 3:9–10, that once again God promises to generously bless those who first generously give to him?

Some might ask, "Isn't that kind of a prosperity gospel where people are promised they'll get rich if they give?" No, this is not a prosperity gospel, this is the generosity gospel. There's a difference.

Those who embrace the prosperity gospel give to get.

Those who embrace the generosity gospel give to give.

Will God bless those who give? Yes! He promises he will. Does that mean that everyone who gives will drive a Rolls, vacation in Italy, or be crypto millionaires? Of course not. But God does bless those who are generous.

Because God's blessings are eternal, he has a value system totally different from the world's. In Isaiah 55:9, he says, "As the heavens are higher than the earth, so are my ways higher than your ways and my thoughts than your thoughts." His ways and thoughts redefine what blessing and generosity look like.

When you pre-decide to put God first in your finances, he promises to open the floodgates and pour out blessing on you. And thankfully, what he provides is much broader and much better than just monetary blessings. His blessings may or may not be financial, but God is the ultimate giver and assures us he will prove himself faithful.

As Jesus said, it's more blessed to give than to receive.

The Pivot

If you make the changes necessary to put God first by pre-deciding to live by his generosity plan, it will change the cycle. Remember the typical cycle?

Spending all or more than we make, being tight financially, living paycheck to paycheck, freaking out and worrying and worrying and worrying, and always wishing we had money to give is not working for anyone. It's time to break the cycle.

When we put God first by pre-deciding to give to him first, we create a different cycle.

We decide to trust God, so we give back to him our first 10 percent.

We give God our first and best. We trust God to bless the rest.

God then proves himself faithful, and that strengthens our faith. This is when it gets powerful, because in place of fear, God builds our faith. When faith replaces worry, we experience the blessing of generosity and find ourselves thinking about giving even more (instead of wishing we could give something).

Generosity allows faith to replace fear.
Generosity allows blessing to replace worry.

The faith cycle changes your life and allows you to change the world.

Let me tell you about some of my friends who pre-decided to put God first by tithing and, as their faith grew, by growing their planned generosity.

- I have a friend who pre-decided to give, above his tithe, fifty dollars a month as the Spirit leads. He's always on the lookout for opportunities God gives him to bless someone and has budgeted fifty dollars a month to do so.
- I know someone else who pre-decided to continually increase their level of generosity by 1 percent every year, starting from 10 percent.
- I have another friend who pre-decided to give a specific portion of their tax return each year to the YouVersion Bible App, to help fund getting God's Word to the world.
- I also know a couple who have been so strategic with the money God's given them, and who so passionately believe it's better to give than receive, that they give 50 percent of their business profits to ministries around the world.

Do you know what all those people have in common? They are more blessed. They are more joyful. They are more fulfilled. And they are making a bigger difference in this world.

How does that happen?

Not by accident.

Generous people plan to be generous.

What might happen if you put ten dollars, maybe twenty, in your pocket and then ask God to show you who needs it more than you?

You can find out for yourself, if you pre-decide.

5.4

Generous People Round Up

Years ago I went to a restaurant and the server was not friendly. When I say "not friendly," I mean she was *not* friendly.

When it came time to pay the bill, I felt the Spirit prompting me to round up and bless her with a big tip. It wasn't an enormous amount, but I followed that leading and gave her a bigger tip than usual. I paid, left, and forgot all about it.

A while later a friend at church told me about meeting someone who waited on me at a restaurant. This waitress admitted she was not friendly to me because she knew who I was and did not like God or our church. She intentionally did a bad job, so when she saw I gave her a big tip, she was confused. She said it softened her heart that I blessed her despite her being rude. Soon after, some painful things happened in her life. Hurting, she was hit with the thought, *Well, I guess I could give that church a try.* She did, and her life was changed.

It all started with a small, simple rounding up.

The second pre-decision generous people make is to round up.

I love Proverbs 21:26, in which Solomon contrasts the sluggard to the righteous: "All day long he craves and craves, but the righteous gives and does not hold back" (ESV). To be honest, I'm not exactly sure what a sluggard is, but it's a gross-sounding word and I don't want to be one. I want to be righteous, which means I need to give and not hold back.

We round up.

Jesus teaches rounding up. He says in Matthew 5:41, "If anyone forces you to go one mile, go with them two miles." And "If someone wants to take your shirt, give him your Members Only jacket too." (That's my own personal 1987 paraphrase of verse 40.)

Don't just give what's expected. Give more. Do more. Round up.

You see this over and over in the Bible.

The Good Samaritan was walking along when he saw a man who was beaten and left for dead. He put some oil and bandages on him and took him to a hotel. At that point he didn't say, "All right, I did what I could. Good luck." No. "The next day he took out two denarii and gave them to the innkeeper. 'Look after him,' he said, 'and when I return, I will reimburse you for any extra expense you may have'" (Luke 10:35).

He rounded up.

Zacchaeus was a chief tax collector for the Romans—not that different from a mafioso—who strong-armed the locals into giving him their money. Then he encountered Jesus and his life was transformed by grace. He announced that he was going to make things right with the people he wronged. So did he give back what he had taken? Nope. He rounded up. "Here and now I give half of my possessions to the poor, and if I have cheated anybody out of anything, I will pay back four times the amount" (Luke 19:8).

Think about that! *Four* times the amount. He was so overwhelmed by the blessings of God's grace that he felt compelled to give extravagantly to others.

Generous people pre-decide to round up, because being generous isn't just something they do, it's who they are. So they plan to be generous. They stand firm in their generosity. They strategically orient their lives around the value of blessing others. When God blesses the generous with more, they say:

> We will not just raise our standard of living.
> We will raise our standard of giving.

The next time you're figuring out how much tip to give, bless your server by rounding up. If you are making a meal for someone, also make an appetizer and a dessert. If you give someone a gift card so they can go on a dinner date, offer to take care of their kids too.

I saw a stunning display of rounding-up generosity on a mission trip to an impoverished nation. If you've never been, picture homes with dirt floors and no electricity, running water, or indoor plumbing. We were at a woman's home, sitting outside on logs, when she gave me some meat she had cooked. I told her, "Thank you so much," and then our translator said, "Let me tell you the story behind this." At that time, my wife was on a no-meat kick, so I had joked in a sermon at our church about needing meat. *A man needs meat! Someone get me some meat!* Well, somehow this woman had heard about that before we came to her country. Our translator explained, "She would not have eaten meat herself in months and months. But when she heard you were coming and really needed meat, she saved up so she could bless you."

Wow.

Let that sink in. A woman who had almost nothing sacrificed to bless me, a man who has almost everything. I could barely sleep that night and I still get emotional reflecting on her extravagant gift.

It reminds me of the Macedonian Christians we read about in the Bible. "Now I want you to know, dear brothers and sisters, what God in his kindness has done through the churches in Macedonia. They are being tested by many troubles, and they are very poor. But they are also filled with abundant joy, which has overflowed in rich generosity. For I can testify that they gave not only what they could afford, but far more. And they did it of their own free will. They begged us again and again for the privilege of sharing" (2 Cor. 8:1–4 NLT).

Did you catch that? They did not think, *When we have more, then we'll give more. One day we hope to be generous.* No, they gave more when they had less.

Generous people round up.

There was a gentleman at our church who was a tither—he worshiped God by giving him the first 10 percent—but heard some teaching on generosity and thought, *Why have I stopped at 10 percent? I could give more.* He decided to round up by giving 15 percent of his income instead of 10 percent. He was blessed by God and wanted to be a blessing.

The next week he was at our Saturday-night church service led by a guest worship leader named Mindy. After he got home, he was struck by the thought, *I am supposed to give to that lady who led worship tonight.* He tried but could not shake the idea. He felt like it was from God.

He went back to church the next day and handed a pastor an envelope full of cash, explaining that he felt like he heard from God and needed the money to be given to the worship leader from the night before. What he didn't know was that Mindy's husband, Bryce, had a very rare blood disease. Because of it, Mindy devoted her attention to him and couldn't work full-time. They had several kids. The weekend that she led worship, their family was in a very difficult time. Bryce was about to get a stem-cell transplant.

When Mindy and Bryce received the money, they wept. This was a direct, immediate, and personal confirmation that God saw their pain and cared about their need. God loved this family so much he prompted a total stranger to give what seemed like a random extravagant gift. God met their need. He is so good!

But Mindy and Bryce weren't the only ones blessed in this miracle moment. When the man who'd given the money heard the story about their financial need, he was absolutely blown away that God had spoken to him in such a specific way. He knew beyond a shadow of a doubt that he had heard from God. He cried with joy knowing that God had used him to change someone's life.

And it happened because he was generous. Because he had a plan, and rounded up.

Standing Firm in Generosity

If you're having trouble picturing yourself living generously, I understand. I am not a generous person by nature. When it comes to money, I was raised to conserve at all costs, and not to give.

In my book *Winning the War in Your Mind*, I wrote in detail about growing up with an extreme scarcity mindset. After learning about the Great Depression, I lived with an irrational and overwhelming fear that the economy would come crashing down again. While other kids were stressing about flunking spelling tests, I would lie awake at night worried my family would be on the street digging for food in garbage cans.

When I'd get birthday cash or get paid for babysitting or mowing a yard, I'd feel slightly more secure. Since I suspected the banks weren't trustworthy (a fear I learned from my depression-surviving grandma), I'd hide the cash under the carpet in my secret money-stashing spot in the back corner of my closet. My little loot lump buried behind my dirty laundry gave me the illusion of security. If the economy did crash, at least I'd have enough cash to get by for a few weeks.

So when I became a Christian in college, God had a lot of work to do on my dysfunctional relationship with money. My first big hurdle came when I learned about tithing and read tough verses like Luke 16:13, where Jesus says, "You cannot serve both God and money." Giving 10 percent felt like losing a significant portion of my security. That's when he showed me clearly:

I was putting my trust in money and not in God.

God was about to teach me something new.

After working all summer teaching tennis, I had made what felt like a lot of money for a twenty-year-old. Convicted for the first time that I should trust God with my finances, I distinctly remember my hand shaking as I nervously wrote my first tithe check. (If you don't know what a check is, don't worry, a couple of my grown kids didn't either. Just take a moment and thank God for modern technology.)

After worshiping and honoring God with my very first tithe, I was surprised by an inexplicable peace in my heart that money couldn't buy. And, just like he promised, God proved himself faithful by providing for me in a way that could only have been from him. Thirty-six years later, I've never not tithed.

But I want to be honest and tell you that overcoming my fear-driven mindset with money has been extremely difficult. Looking back, I now realize my problem wasn't a money problem. My problem was a spiritual problem.

> I was trusting what I could see instead of trusting what God had said.

As I've trusted God and given generously, I've found that what Jesus promises is truer than I ever anticipated. I've learned the truth behind verses like Matthew 7:24, where Jesus says, "Therefore everyone who hears these words of mine and puts them into practice is like a wise man who built his house on the rock."

It really is more blessed to give than to receive.

Before long I started rounding up by giving some offerings above my tithe. Then I married Amy, and she was more generous by nature. Even though our income was limited and our finances tight in the early years, she helped me grow even more in the joy of generosity.

When we were starting out, we used the envelope system for budgeting our money. At the beginning of each month, we'd put cash for groceries in one envelope, cash for gas in another, and cash for incidentals in another. We had an envelope for every expense.

One month, when we still had ten days until payday, we ran to the grocery store with only sixty dollars left. We were shopping in the cereal aisle, inspired by my childhood heroes—the Trix Rabbit, Sugar Bear, and Cap'n Crunch[30]—when we saw a lady with four young children who was obviously going through a very difficult time. I suddenly felt like maybe we were supposed to give her our grocery money. Knowing we needed food, I tried to shake the feeling. That's when Amy looked at me, and then at the single mom, and asked, "Are you thinking what I'm thinking?"

I approached the woman. "Ma'am," I said, trying my best not to make it awkward, "I, uh, I really feel like, uh, I can't explain it, but uh, well, I feel like we are supposed to give you this." I handed her the remainder of our month's meal money.

When we handed her the cash, she tried to refuse. We insisted, and she broke down crying. She hugged us. Cried more. Hugged us again. Cried some more.

God used our small gift to bless her.

God used our small gift to bless *us* even more.

When I got home, I cried and cried. My tears weren't for her. They were for me. Why had I been so selfish for so many years? What blessings had I missed out on? God was doing a work in me. And we pre-decided not only to tithe but to reorient our lives around generosity.

A couple of years later, when Amy and I started Life.Church, we felt God's nudge to give a really big financial gift. Essentially, God prompted us to round up. We emptied our checking and savings accounts, joyfully giving all we could.

As we continued to grow in a desire for generosity, we initiated what we call "get one, give one." It started with shirts. If you get a new shirt, you give away a shirt you have. Then we added get a pair of pants, give a pair of pants. From there we upgraded to furniture. Get a chair, give a chair. Then we included appliances. Get a refrigerator, give a refrigerator. Then we were going to buy a car. I thought, *Get a car, give a car? No. Get a car and sell a car to someone for a fair price.* It felt like too much to give away, but God worked on me. It was like he was saying, *Give your car, Craig. And round up. Fill it with gas. Get it detailed. Deliver it to the person instead of having them come pick it up.* Part of me thought this was crazy, but the other part of me couldn't say no to the idea. Am I sure that thought was from God? No, but it sure sounded like him. Remember, he says it's more blessed to give than to receive.

I have learned God is faithful, and the old cliché is true:

> You cannot outgive God.

To this day, we are careful to live beneath our means, not because I am still driven by fear but because we want to give as much as possible. To quote my friend Dave Ramsey:[31]

> We are going to live like no one else so we can give like no one else.

If you want to be generous someday, start being generous today. If you want to be generous when you have more, learn to be generous when you have less.

Pre-decide: I will be generous.

Generous is not just what we do, it's who we are. We were made in the image of a generous God who gave his Son for us. Our generous God tells us it's more blessed to give than to receive. We will be happier. We will better represent our God. We will make a bigger impact and leave a better legacy.

Knowing that generosity never happens by accident, we plan and stand firm in our generosity.

We pre-decide: I am generous.

PART 5 EXERCISES

1. On a scale of 1 to 10, how would you rate your selfishness today? Explain your score.
2. What is the most generous action you have ever taken? (It doesn't have to be financial.) How did your generosity make you feel?
3. On a scale of 1 to 10, how would you rate your generosity today? Explain your score.
4. Do you see any connection between your scores on selfishness and generosity? Explain.
5. Consider this statement from p. 142: "We want to be generous but don't think we can." Is this true for you? Does anything keep you from being more generous?
6. Do you agree with this statement from p. 144: "More money doesn't change who you are, it just reveals who you are." Why or why not?
7. Is there a situation in which you feel compelled to be generous or to meet a need but haven't followed through on it yet? What steps can you take to obey that prompting?
8. Reflect on the difference between giving and being generous. Do you feel a gap between your giving and your generosity? Explain.
9. Give a brief description of your financial plan.
10. Which of these two financial cycles best fits you? Explain.

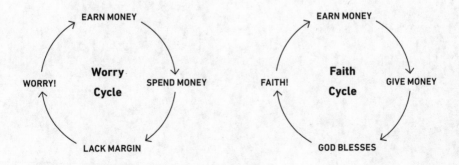

I Will Be Consistent

Therefore, my dear brothers and sisters, stand firm. Let nothing move you. Always give yourselves fully to the work of the Lord, because you know that your labor in the Lord is not in vain.

—1 CORINTHIANS 15:58

6.1

Inconsistent Anonymous

Hi. My name is Craig, and I am inconsistent.

It's a little embarrassing (though not as embarrassing as getting stuck attempting to scale the church walls), and I would love for it to be anonymous, but I'm just going to put it out there.

Would you like to take a seat at this meeting of Inconsistent (Not-So) Anonymous?

If you struggle with inconsistency, you probably have good intentions. The real issue is follow-through. You might be inconsistent in any of these areas:

- eating
- exercising
- parenting
- saving money
- calling your mom
- praying
- reading the Bible
- journaling
- showing up on time

You may be thinking, *The only thing I'm consistent at is being inconsistent!*

Sorry, joking about it is probably too painful to be funny. The truth is our inconsistency is insidious. We read in Scripture, "A person without self-control is like a city with broken-down walls" (Prov. 25:28 NLT). Without self-control, without consistency, we are vulnerable to temptations, harmful addictions, destructive behavior, and our enemy's spiritual attacks. Inconsistency opens the door to all kinds of toxic issues. It infects your life, hurts your health, wrecks your finances, kills your confidence, and interrupts the intimacy you should have *with* others and the influence you could have *on* others.

If your life is not what you want, it's likely because you've been infected with inconsistency.

I get you.

There are so many areas of my life where I have been embarrassingly inconsistent. For now I'll share just one.

Praying Together *Sounds* Easy

Hi. My name is Craig, and I have always believed it's important to pray with my wife.

It's been proven that praying together is great for the health of your marriage. In America about 50 percent of first marriages end in divorce, and 78 percent of second marriages end in divorce. But fewer than 1 percent of couples who pray together daily end their marriages.[32] Pause to let that sink in. Praying together may be the strongest marriage protection possible. Yet only 11 percent of couples pray together.

Plus, I'm a pastor. There are some things pastors should not do, and others they should.

Pastors should not say at a funeral, "Ashes to ashes, dust to dust, sure hope this coffin doesn't rust!" (I may know that from experience. In my defense, I was only twenty-two at the time.)

Pastors should pray with their spouses.

Right? It seems like the bare minimum.

Because we should, I always wanted to pray with Amy, but for years and years we were incredibly inconsistent. ("Inconsistent" is a generous way to say we prayed together almost never.)

I would feel convicted and tell Amy, "I love you. And I love God. And I'm a *pastor* who loves you and loves God. We should pray together. We're really gonna do it this time!" And we would—for three days. Then we'd stop. A few months would go by, and my guilt would reemerge, so I would announce again, "Amy, get ready to pray together, 'cause we're doing this!" and we would start again, then stop.

Why?

While I could give you a long list of excuses, I'll give you just three.

1. *It takes Amy so long to start praying.* When I'm ready to go, she's still doing some kind of pre-prayer breathing exercise that takes forever. I'm like, "Amy, can we get started? Amy, your breathing is fine. We're trying to get better at praying together, not breathing." One time I think I heard the voice of God say, "Amy, he's right. Let's get this prayer going." (Amy denies hearing anything. I think she was too busy breathing.)

2. *Amy likes to pray longer than I do.* When I say, "Amy, we're doing this," I assume we're going to pray together for a few minutes. She puts a roast in the oven and tells me we need to be done praying by the time it's ready.

3. *Every time we start to pray, something happens.* With six kids, there's always something. "Something" could mean fluid coming out of a kid's body, or a kid's head getting stuck between the stair rails, or a Polly Pocket getting flushed down the toilet, or exactly $1.25 of nickels getting swallowed just when a kid needs her piggybank coins back to buy ice cream.

To be fair, if you are reading between the lines, yes, Amy was always willing for us to pray together. But she was also following my lead. I knew we should pray together, but we rarely, if ever, did.

I have been inconsistent.

Why Don't I Do What I Want to Do?

Have you been inconsistent? There might be certain spiritual disciplines you've wanted to practice, or you desperately desired to take better care of your health, or you decided to disciple your kid, or stretch regularly, or keep a gratitude journal, and yet you have been incredibly inconsistent.

Again, I get you.

It gives me strange comfort to know that one of the heroes of our faith, a guy who wrote a big portion of the New Testament, also struggled with inconsistency. The apostle Paul confesses, "I don't really understand myself, for I want to do what is right, but I don't do it. Instead, I do what I hate. . . . I want to do what is right, but I can't. I want to do what is good, but I don't. I don't want to do what is wrong, but I do it anyway" (Rom. 7:15, 18–19 NLT).

Paul gets us.

How many times have you thought, *I don't understand myself. I don't know why I do what I do. Why don't I do the good I want to do? Why do I keep doing the bad I don't want to do?*

Want to know who else has thought that?

Everyone!

Our Inconsistent Anonymous meeting is filled with participants who don't want to be there but know they need to be.

We try to be lighthearted about it, but, honestly, the consequences of our inconsistency can be catastrophic.

If you know that your consistency matters but find yourself being inconsistent, if you're tired of having good intentions but falling short again and again, it's time to pre-decide:

I will be consistent.

Speaking of consistent, if you've read some of my more recent books, you will notice slight overlap with a few topics in the upcoming chapters. I am constantly reminded that these areas of mindset, attitude, and decisions are some of our greatest challenges in life and faith. Zig Ziglar teaches about the power of repetition, "We have to hear something sixteen times to get the complete message. Hearing it over and over can make decisions change into commitment."[33] I believe that, too, so my choice to repeat some truths is intentional.

Like Zig says, it's time to "make decisions change into commitment," then learn how to live out that commitment.

You can.

And when you do, your consistency will change everything.

6.2

The Power of Consistency

What is the one quality you need to live out your decisions to be ready, devoted, faithful, influential, and generous?

If there's a quality that is most important to the trajectory of the rest of your life, to your spiritual strength, ministry impact, physical health, relational intimacy, work success, and financial potential, what do you think it is?

I have good news.

It's not any of these:

- *Genetics.* You know that. You can think of siblings with the same genetics who have lived different lives.
- *Background.* You know of people who overcame challenging backgrounds to experience success.
- *Appearance.* Could you name a not-so-attractive person with no fashion sense who is killing it in life? Yes, you can. (But maybe you shouldn't name names.)
- *Intelligence or education.* We all know smart people with lots of degrees who are still struggling in life.

That's good news because you can't change your genetics or your background, there's only so much you can do about your appearance, and there's not a magic intelligence-increasing pill on sale at the pharmacy.

So what *is* the essential quality?

Consistency.

And right now, you're thinking, *Well, I'm screwed.*

Am I right? As we've already established, you're not going to win any gold medals when it comes to consistency.

So many of us are incredibly inconsistent and we need help to become consistent, to convert our good intentions into good follow-through.

Why?

Because people with good intentions make promises, but people with consistency make progress.

No One's a Natural

Wouldn't you love to be amazing at something? Like world-class amazing?

I've spoken many times over the years about Malcolm Gladwell, a journalist who spent years studying successful people. He wanted to learn: Why are they successful? Are they naturally gifted? Did they inherit supergenes from their parents? Are they just lucky?

What did he find?

Ten thousand hours.

In his book *Outliers: The Story of Success*, Gladwell writes that, across the board, people who are great at something put in ten thousand hours of practice. Their greatness was the result of consistency.

We don't assume that. We tend to think some people are just better than the rest of us.

There's a baseball book called *The Boys of Summer* about the 1955 Brooklyn Dodgers. The author describes Dodger George Shuba as having a swing "as natural as a smile." Wow. How lucky to have a natural swing! Except George Shuba swung a weighted bat at home six hundred times a day every day. That's more than sixteen thousand practice swings a month.[34] Was he a natural? No.

He was consistent.

Successful people do consistently what other people do occasionally.

Successful people do over and over what other people do every now and then. Consistent action creates consistent results.

It's not what we do occasionally that makes the difference, it's what we do consistently. We are what we do consistently.

There's a great example from the Bible.

Around 605 BC, about eighteen years after invading and destroying Jerusalem, the Babylonians came in and abducted a lot of Jewish boys. They picked the best and brightest, typically about twelve years old, with the goal of indoctrinating them. They educated these boys and taught them their values so they might become future leaders in Babylon.

Among the group, Daniel stood out. King Darius noticed his unusual consistency and decided to promote him. "The king made plans to place him over the entire empire" (Dan. 6:3 NLT).

Some of the other leaders felt threatened by Daniel's ascension, so they wanted to dig up dirt on him and get him canceled. They talked to his exes and scrolled through his old social media posts. "Let's see what he tweeted seven years ago." "Let's see if he's posted any photos on Instagram of himself at a rave." "Has he voted wrong? Cyberbullied? Gaslighted? Said something racist or politically incorrect? Practiced nepotism or cannibalism?"

They tried to find fault in his character, "but they couldn't find anything to criticize or condemn. He was faithful, always responsible, and completely trustworthy" (Dan. 6:4 NLT). They couldn't find fault because Daniel was consistent.

Realizing the only way to get to Daniel was through his devotion to God, they hatched a plan. They went to the king and said, "Yo, Darius. We've got an idea for you. And, by the way, have we mentioned that you're the man? That you're the GOAT! That you look awesome in those shoes! That you're the fastest at solving a Rubik's Cube? Oh yeah, and you always smell good! Anyway, we have an idea. Since you personify awesome-sauce, people should pray only to you. Right? So why don't you issue a decree that if anyone prays to any god besides you in the next thirty days, they'll get thrown into the lions' den?"

The king replied, "Thank you. You're right. I am awesome-sauce, I do look good in these shoes, and people should pray only to me. So let's make the decree: anyone who prays to any god other than me in the next thirty days will be thrown into the lions' den."

Remember, Daniel was devoted to God *and* being consistent. So what did Daniel do when he discovered he was now prohibited from praying to his God? "But when Daniel learned that the law had been signed, he went home and knelt down as usual in his upstairs room, with its windows open toward Jerusalem. He prayed three times a day, just as he had always done, giving thanks to his God" (Dan. 6:10 NLT).

Daniel did what he always did. Not something different. Not something new. Not something driven by fear. Daniel continued to consistently pursue the heart of God, three times a day, just as he'd always done. He thought ahead and continued to push his life forward in the direction he wanted, not letting outside forces stop him.

The leaders had not been able to find fault in Daniel because he was consistent. Now they *could* accuse him because he was consistent. They went to the king and told him, "Your honorable awesome-sauce, master of the Rubik's Cube, Daniel disobeyed your decree. You have to throw him into the lions' den."

Remember, the king was a Daniel fanboy, but he had to stand by his word, so he threw Daniel into a pit with hungry lions.

Yikes. End of story. Game over. Do not pass Go, do not collect $200. Stick a fork in him, he's done.

You'd think.

But God sent an angel to close the mouths of the lions. "And when Daniel was lifted from the den, no wound was found on him, because he had trusted in his God" (Dan. 6:23).

I'm hit by those words: "Because he had trusted in his God." I feel like I trust God, a lot, but I'm not sure if I have that kind of trust. (I was pretty nervous when I encountered a bobcat in my driveway! How confident would I be in a lions' den?)

I want to be more like Daniel. You might too. So here's a question for us: When did Daniel learn to trust God?

It was not in the lions' den. It was kneeling to pray three times a day, "as usual," in his upstairs room with the window wide open, "just as he had always done."

Why did Daniel have an incredibly vibrant, close relationship with God? Why was he so successful, confident, and bold in his leadership?

Why did he exhibit such unwavering, unbending, unshakable faith, such that he's a hero of the Bible?

And what about his story makes us want a deeper relationship with God and more faith and success?

Daniel prayed consistently.

We pray occasionally.

> It's not what we do occasionally that makes a difference.
> It's what we do consistently that matters.

If we are going to stick to our decisions, honor God, become everything we're meant to become, and live the life he has for us, we have to grow in our consistency.

And we can.

My wife and I now pray together almost every day. There are things I used to do inconsistently but today do consistently.

What happened?

I learned three game-changing principles that changed my life, and I am so excited to share them with you.

6.3

Start with Why

I want to get you thinking about your *what*. But more important, first, we need to talk about your *why*. A weak *what* can detour your pursuit of your goal. A weak *why* will keep you from pursuing it in the first place.

> A weak *what* is a problem. A weak *why* is a deal killer.

Your *why* is your first and most important domino. You've got to start with *why*.

Right now, you're wondering, *Whaaat?*

I'll explain with an example.

So many people want to get into better shape but don't have enough motivation. That's only one of their obstacles. Another? Their goal (or their *what*) isn't clear. What does it even mean to be in better shape?

- To a bride-to-be, it means looking good in her wedding dress.
- To her future groom, it might mean looking good with her by the pool on their honeymoon.
- To the groom's best man, it could mean bigger biceps.
- To the bride's maid of honor, it might be smaller thighs.
- To the mother of the bride, it might be getting her hormones aligned.
- To the father of the groom, it might mean getting his cholesterol down.

Not only do you need to be clear on what you want to accomplish, but you also need to know why it's important. You might have a *what*, but not a clear *why*.

I get it.

About fifteen years ago I was at the gym working out when my buddy Bart walked in. Bart has the kind of physique that makes most guys not want to show their faces (or, more specifically, their bodies) at the gym. At the time, I had what Amy affectionately called a "dad bod." (I told her I preferred "father figure.") Bart had what I'd call a "wow I really wish I had ripped muscles and abs like that" bod.

"So tell me about your workout, dude," I asked Bart, trying not to sound pathetic. Looking back, I'm guessing people had asked him that question no fewer than 43,832 times. He clearly had a strategy when he responded, "Why are you asking?"

Not prepared for the classic question-counterquestion move, I hesitated. I looked down at my feet, which were also not in ideal shape, and muttered, "You know, bro, like, I just wanna get in better shape." Little did I know I had stepped right into his trap. Smiling as if he enjoyed the hunt, Bart asked, "And what exactly do you mean by 'get in better shape'?"

Still off-balance, I tried to look confident and responded, "Ya know, get toner." My voice trailed off the moment I said "toner." Why did I say "toner"?

Then my friend went for the jugular. "That's great that you want to focus on your fitness." He paused, ready to set the hook deeper. "But why?"

Why?

Why?

What did he mean by why? Why was he asking me why? Why does anyone want to get into better shape? Why does he need to know why? Wasn't it enough to just kind of want to be better?

Bart taught me two unforgettable lessons:

1. If you aren't clear on your what, you'll never accomplish it. You cannot do what you do not define.
2. If your why isn't strong enough, you won't accomplish your what. Why? (Pun intended.) Because your why drives your what.

We need to start with why.

Why did Daniel pray consistently? He was devoted to God. That led to his decision to connect with the heart of God three times a day.

Let's talk about New Year's resolutions. Why do so many people start with good intentions but fail to follow through? A study of eight hundred million Americans found that New Year's resolutions die, on average, by January 19.[35] The reason? Their resolutions are the result of desire, not devotion. A desire can feel strong, but it's typically shallow and fleeting. Devotion to a why goes deeper, and without a compelling why, you are not likely to stay consistent.

Why do I say most New Year's resolutions are the result of desire, not devotion? Because New Year's resolutions start on New Year's. Think about that. You waited until January 1.

You had a moment when you thought, "I should lose ten pounds," or "I want to quit smoking," or "I ought to start exercising," or "Maybe it's time to get an emotional support lizard."[36] So you decided you would—on January 1. The day you felt that desire might have been September 29 or November 4, but you put off acting on it until January 1.

Why did you wait? Because you didn't have a strong enough why. If you had a real why, you wouldn't have thought, *On January 1, I am going to start eating well, but until then I am going to eat anything and everything!*

And yes, you will choose the salad on January 1, but by January 19 you're back to cuckoo for Cocoa Puffs for breakfast, fettuccine Alfredo for lunch, and chocolate cake for dinner. Why did your resolution fail?

Your why was not compelling enough.

If you had a legit why, you wouldn't wait until January 1. Right? If your doctor tells you in October that you have severe diabetes and need to stop eating sugar or you will die, you won't say, "Okay, then, Ben & Jerry's ice cream for the next three months! Then I'll quit when it's a new year." No, you'd have a strong why and it would compel you to decide and be consistent now.

If you want to grow in consistency, start with why.

What change do you want to see in your life?

You might want to be closer to God, have a better marriage, quit a bad habit, have closer friendships, or have more financial stability.

Great. All good things.

But *why?*

What is your why? You have to start with why. If not, you will start strong but struggle with follow-through, again. (Just like my praying with Amy, I had to get past what to my why.)

So what's your why?

You may want to be closer to God. Why? You might answer, "I feel like I'm supposed to. I mean, I'm a Christian. And isn't that what good church people do?"

No, that why is not compelling enough to sustain consistency. But when you become sick of the devil's distractions, tired of his pulling you away from God, convinced God created you for his glory, determined to serve him wholeheartedly, and committed to helping generations come to know his grace and goodness, then *that* just might create a consistency that drives devotion!

You want to have a better marriage? Good. But why? "Because my spouse is a jerk and I'm sick of fighting." No. That is a weak why. How about "I made vows to my spouse and to God, and I want to honor them. I want to leave a legacy for my children and grandchildren of what it looks like to have a Jesus-centered, faith-empowered marriage." Yes!

You have a goal of greater financial stability. Why? "'Cause I've got the fifty-five-inch TV but I want the seventy-inch TV. And I want to get Disney+. And there's a new car I've been eyeing." No, that's not a why that will motivate you after your initial burst of energy. A better why? "I refuse to live paycheck to paycheck anymore. I refuse to live the rest of my life like my parents, worrying about whether I can pay the bills. I want financial freedom so I can be generous for God and make a difference in people's lives."

What's your why?

Why-Power over Willpower

Typically, when we make commitments, we rely on willpower to keep them consistently. The problem, as we learned in chapter 1, is that willpower wanes. So when our decision meets resistance—and there will always be resistance—our willpower will eventually give out and we will cave.

That's why we're pre-deciding to do this instead:

Shift from willpower to why-power.

A strong why will make all the difference. You will find that your why trumps excuses and defeats detractors.

When King Darius decreed that those who prayed to God would be fed to the lions, it was not willpower that enabled Daniel to keep praying. It was his why that would not let him stop. (Or, if you're a child of the '90s or an MC Hammer fan, it was his why that made Daniel "too legit to quit.")

Resistance happens. Times will get tough. But take heart:

When you know your why, you will find a way.

Daniel kept praying, and Amy and I started praying together, when we found our why. That's what we had been lacking. My why was always "Well, I'm a pastor. So I'm probably supposed to."

That is a weak, weak, weak *why*.

Then I thought about how everything in our family and ministry depended on the presence and power of God. We needed grace for our marriage, direction for our parenting, wisdom for our leadership. And I knew that Jesus says something powerful happens when people come together and pray in his name. And I realized the devil doesn't take a day off, so I better be seeking God together with my bride every day.

Same with my desire to get into better shape. My first why—wanting to look better—was honestly a weak why. But while reading Scripture, I was reminded that my body is the temple of the Holy Spirit (1 Cor. 6:19). Instead of only trying to look better on the outside, I decided to honor God with what I put on the inside. In the same way I honor him with my finances, or by seeking him in prayer, or by pursuing purity, I would honor God with my body. Suddenly, saying no to the wrong food and saying yes to the right disciplines became so much easier. The right why gave me the motivation to do what I felt God calling me to do.

If you want to become more consistent, define your why. Go deep. Pray. Look within. Tap into your passion.

Start with why.

6.4

Plan to Fail

Now when it comes to my body and my physical health, my why drives my what. Because of that why-power, I now have a clear what:

- a targeted weight range
- a targeted hormone range
- a target for each of my vitals
- types of food I do and don't eat
- times of day I eat and don't eat
- amount of food I eat
- types of snacks that are always on hand
- types of snacks I keep as far away from me as possible because I know I'm vulnerable (hint: it "melts in your mouth and not in your hands")
- weight-training and cardio goals
- a carefully planned supplement regimen
- a targeted time to go to bed and wake up
- an amount of water to drink and when (hint: too late in the day and I will get up three times in the night!)

I have a clear what. I have pre-decided what to eat, what not to eat, and how to maximize my body to perform at the highest level.

What's my why?

I'll tell you what it's not. I'm not planning to compete in the Fifty-and-Over Pastors' Bodybuilding Division.

My why is to honor God with my body. No matter my age, I will be faithful to strengthen the body God gave me so I can serve him with all my mind, soul, and strength.

Am I living this out perfectly? Of course not. Why? I'm human. I don't plan to be perfect. I plan to fail. And I would encourage you to as well.

> If you want to succeed, plan to fail.

I know that seems counterintuitive and may even sound contradictory, but it's true. One reason we fail in our commitments is because we don't plan to fail.

Perfectionism is a roadblock to great decision-making.[37] If you focus on the potential to make mistakes, it's easy to give up or not try. As Ryan says in *The Office*, "I'm such a perfectionist that I'd kinda rather not do it at all than do a crappy version."[38]

> The problem with perfection is that it's not possible.

What holds us back isn't perfection but the illusion of perfection. We demand perfection of ourselves and assume everyone else is perfect. But the reality is no one is doing anything perfectly.

Think about Daniel. We read that he prayed three times a day, "just as he had always done." Do you think he ever missed one of his three daily prayer times?

I bet he did.

Why?

Because he was human, and no one is perfect.

As a real person in the real world, Daniel had to deal with the same frustrating circumstances we do. You know there was a time when the king asked him to stay late for work, or there was a big game on and his friends ordered pizza and wings, or he got stuck in traffic (the camels were at a standstill; it was nose-to-butt as far as the eye could see). There must have been a few bad days when he missed one of his three prayer times. So what did he do?

He went right back to praying three times a day.

Psychologists consider an all-or-nothing mindset a debilitating cognitive distortion[39] that impedes great decision-making, and too often we're held back by it. When we fail, we think of ourselves as a failure. *I failed, so forget it. I quit.*

No!

There's a big difference between being consistent and being perfect. You are going to fail. Everyone fails. That means you won't be perfect. But your goal is not perfection. Your goal is consistency. You're wise to plan to fail and give yourself grace when you do. That way you can keep going and stay consistent.

Since Amy and I started praying together consistently, I've had people ask me for advice on it. Others ask for help praying with their kids. I always offer three things:

1. Keep it simple.
2. Keep it short.
3. If you miss one day, don't miss two.

Why keep it simple? Because if you make it complicated, you probably won't do it.

Why keep it short? Because if the goal seems intimidating, you won't try. (Do you have to keep it short? No! You can pray as long as you want. But your odds of praying long go up if your standard is to pray short.) Keep the bar low at first to get you started and make showing up a success.

Why do I say "If you miss a day, don't miss two"? Because you *are* going to miss a day. You'll have that crazy day when your water heater dies, or your mother calls and asks you to explain how to use that confusing app on her phone again, or your air-guitar band finally makes it to the quarterfinals. Plan on missing a day. Praying with Amy, I have given myself permission to miss occasionally. I need that because I *will* miss occasionally. When it happens, I realize it's part of the process and make sure I don't miss two days. One day is an exception. No big deal. Two or three is a pattern. So if you miss one day, don't miss two.

The illusion of perfection can keep us from getting started. We think, *I'll never be able to do it right, so I might as well not even try.* No. We're not going to be perfect, but we *can* be consistent.

There are two passages in the book of Hebrews that can give us inspiration, confidence, and hope to be consistent, because we serve a Savior who is perfect. The first is Hebrews 4:14–16: "So then, since we have a great High Priest who has entered heaven, Jesus the Son of God, let us hold firmly to what we believe. This High Priest of ours understands our weaknesses, for he faced all of the same testings we do, yet he did not sin. So let us come boldly to the throne of our gracious God. There we will receive his mercy, and we will find grace to help us when we need it most" (NLT).

The second is the picture of perfection *and* consistency: "Jesus Christ is the same yesterday and today and forever" (Heb. 13:8).

I began taking jujitsu classes with my sons. It's very challenging to get a higher-ranking belt in jujitsu. You start with a white belt, then earn blue, then purple, then brown, then black. In between each belt, you receive stripes along the way. On the fifth stripe you get a belt promotion.

My instructor asked me, "Which belt do you think is the most difficult to get?" I answered, "Obviously, the black belt." He said, "No. The most difficult is the white belt because most people never start."

So true! And that's exactly where I had been for years. I wanted to do jujitsu but was afraid I was too old or wouldn't be good enough.

He then asked, "What is a black belt?" I said, "That's someone you run from." I thought it was a good answer. I had trained with several guys with black belts. They were lethal. You run from them. He didn't laugh when he said, "No, a black belt is a white belt that was consistent." Ohhh. I like that. A black belt is a white belt who refused to give up.

After hearing that, guess how many lessons I missed?

The answer rhymes with hero.

Until I was injured. Of course I was injured. I'm in my midfifties, rolling on a sweaty mat with twentysomething-year-old guys who look like a cross between a pit bull and a Mack truck.

Do you know what happened after I got injured and had surgery? I missed practice. Perfection was destroyed.

Just like when you broke your diet and ate the wrong thing, or overslept and didn't work out, or bought something stupid in the middle of trying to get out of debt, or looked at something you shouldn't have looked at, or lost your daily reading streak on the YouVersion Bible App.

I was injured and couldn't do jujitsu for more than two months. Then what? Then I was healthy again and went back to the gym to start a new streak.

But what about being perfect?

I was never perfect and never going to be perfect. That's an illusion. I always planned on failing, so missing two months because of an injury perfectly fit my plan. I did plan on being consistent, and as soon as I could, I went back to consistent. I had to, because I had a deep why, and consistency is the essential quality.

It is for you, too, so don't get caught up trying to be perfect. That doesn't work for anyone. But consistency works for everyone.

6.5

Fall in Love with the Process

Want to hear some potential book title ideas? I will warn you, they are going to sound boring. Here goes:

- *Boring Is the New Exciting!*
- *Bore Your Way to the Top!*
- *If You Ain't Boring, You Ain't Scoring!*
- *Bore Your Way to Success!*
- *Bored Stiff? More Like Bored Awesome!*

Boring may be boring. But boring is actually a much better strategy than obsessing about results. Why? Because focusing on results is the downfall of people who want to be consistent. Yes, goals are sexy. But obsessing about them causes inconsistency. So instead we are going to fall in love with the process. The process may seem boring. It's not.

It's going to change your life.

Daniel's three prayers weren't some grueling sessions he had to endure because of a goal he'd put on his vision board. He loved praying because he loved God and the intimacy it created with him.

Daniel worked hard every day not because he hoped to get promoted. He just consistently lived his life in a way that honored God.

Too many of us obsess about the goal. "I've got to lose twenty pounds!" "I need to pay off all of my credit cards!" "I've gotta read through the whole Bible!"

We have this "win" we're going after. We know it will feel amazing to achieve it. The problem is that day may be far off.

- Losing twenty pounds might take you six months.
- Paying off your credit cards could take two years.
- Reading through the Bible may take a whole year.

That's not a bad thing, but if you're obsessed with the goal, it will feel like it's taking forever. If you are focused on your win, every day you still haven't achieved it might feel like you're losing. But if you fall in love with the process, you can win every day.

Isn't that cool? It often takes time before you see the results of consistency. You do the right thing for a few weeks or months, but you still feel out of shape, haven't paid off much of your debt, or haven't reignited those honeymoon feelings with your spouse. That's okay. Success is not when you hit the goal in the future.

> You are successful when you do what you need to do today.

This is another weakness in the typical New Year's resolution. "Get a promotion" or "lose thirty pounds" sound great, but those are goals. How are you going to achieve those goals?

What you need is a process.

Process Precedes Progress

If you can fall in love with that process, the results will follow. As you work your plan and see some progress, you will want to do it consistently every day. And if you do it consistently, you will reach your goal. If, instead, you fall in love with the goal, every day you don't achieve your goal, you will feel like a failure. Eventually you'll get frustrated and quit, never reaching your desired result. Remember this:

> Consistency isn't an event. It's a process.

When I roll with my boys (that's what we jujitsu types call what we do—rolling), my win isn't the next belt. That's likely two years away. My win is when I show up. I love getting to do jujitsu with my sons every day possible. Because of that, I'm consistent. Because I'm consistent, I make progress. Because I make progress, I will get that next belt. (And because I'm making progress and going to the next belt, that bobcat better watch his back. If you think I'm kidding, check out this article about a Brazilian jujitsu-trained jogger who choked out a mountain lion to save his own life.[40])

Consistency Creates Momentum

Jesus' ministry on this planet lasted about three years. In John 17 we are given the words of his prayer before he went to the cross, in which he makes statements like "I have brought you glory," "I have revealed you," and "I protected them." Why was he able to make those statements? Because Jesus was committed to being consistent in the process of bringing salvation to the world. Every day.

I'm sure there were plenty of boring moments sitting around the campfire or walking to the next town or listening to another lecture from the Pharisees. Yet, in the end, Jesus was able to say, "I brought glory to you here on earth by completing the work you gave me to do. Now, Father, bring me into the glory we shared before the world began" (vv. 4–5 NLT).

The process may not be as glamorous as the goal. Some may even call it boring. That's okay. You're going to learn to love boring. And when you do, maybe you can write the book titled *Boring Is the New Exciting!* or *I'm Bored Awesome!* But the process that leads to the goal in our lives can bring glory to God.

6.6

But I Can't

It's time to pre-decide: I will be consistent.

How will you achieve consistency? You will

- start with why,
- plan to fail, and
- fall in love with the process.

I wonder if you are struggling with some self-doubt. You might be thinking, *This sounds great, and I'd love to, but I'm not sure I can. I've tried to be consistent before and it didn't go so well.*

If you aren't sure you'll be consistent, I would tell you that's probably true.

You can't.

On your own.

But you are not on your own.

It Takes Two. (But Three? Even Better!)

When I started my journey toward honoring God consistently with my body, I knew I needed help. (I'd never traded a dad bod for a God-honoring bod before and couldn't find a YouTube video to tell me how.) Since Bart was my closest friend that seemed to know what he was doing, I asked if he'd help me. I didn't expect him to dump the equivalent of a master's degree in nutrition and physical fitness on me over the next few weeks, but that's exactly what he did.

As I engaged in the process toward God-honoring health, suddenly (and strangely) I discovered other people who took the care of their "temples" seriously. (They had always been around, but I'd never noticed.) Without meaning to, I assembled a new group of friends who shared a passion for pursuing peak physical health. This group of fitness-minded friends became my support team. It's not dissimilar to recovering alcoholics. Those who are serious about sobriety find strength in community. They know that alone they are vulnerable, but together they have infinitely better odds.

After starting strong on my newfound diet and fitness strategy, I made immediate progress. But when the initial gains gradually diminished, so did my enthusiasm. That's when quitting looked appealing. As fast as I'd started, I was ready to quit. *This is just too much work. Life is too short to skip dessert. You were doing fine before all of these strict rules. And besides, you are a dad anyway. Dads have dad bods!*

That's when my group of friends stepped in and told me this:

> When you feel like quitting, remember why you started.

There it was again. Remember your why.

Thanks to my likeminded friends who had my back, I continued with the process instead of taking the easy exit. Now it's not just something I hope to do. It's who I am. I am consistent.

I can't do it on my own. But I am not on my own.

You can't on your own, but you are not on your own. One or two supportive friends make all the difference. "Two people are better off than one, for they can help each other succeed. If one person falls, the other can reach out and help. But someone who falls alone is in real trouble. Likewise, two people lying close together can keep each other warm. But how can one be warm alone? A person standing alone can be attacked and defeated, but two can stand back-to-back and conquer. Three are even better, for a triple-braided cord is not easily broken" (Eccl. 4:9–12 NLT).

Solomon wrote those words thousands of years ago, but they are just as true today. Studies have demonstrated the importance of supportive friends in achieving goals,[41] for your mental health, with your ability to manage and overcome challenges that might interrupt your consistency,[42] and in having the coping skills to overcome stress and navigate life's obstacles.[43]

- People do better with diets when they have a community of support, which is one reason WeightWatchers has been around so long.
- People can run farther if they're running with others instead of by themselves.
- When recovering from addiction, people tend to find it's too hard on their own but doing it with others in a program makes it possible.
- People grow best spiritually in community.

The right team can produce an amazing effect called synergy. Synergy is "the interaction of elements that when combined produce a total effect that is greater than the sum of the individual elements or contributions."[44] In short, synergy means we can be better together.

If you remember your why, plan to fail, and fall in love with the process, it will help you to form your team. Assemble your tribe. Gather your troops.

You can't, but with a couple of friends cheering you on and holding you accountable, you can. Two are better than one. Three? Even better.

God Can

We've pre-decided: I will be consistent.

But let's be more precise: With God's help, I will be consistent.

You think you're still not able to be consistent. You're right. Same here.

I can't. God can.

Here's where the rubber meets the road. In what area is God calling you to pre-decide consistency? Does he want you to do any of the following?

- consistently live by a budget
- consistently pay down debt
- consistently pray with your spouse or children
- consistently practice piano, or Spanish, or nunchucks
- consistently attend church or serve in church
- consistently read God's Word
- consistently eat wisely
- consistently avoid porn
- consistently avoid junk food
- consistently read good books

What's it going to be? Don't just state a broad goal. Be clear and specific. You cannot do what you do not define.

Then what will you do? It's simple. You will pre-decide that you are consistent. How will you be consistent?

1. Start with your why.
2. Plan to fail.
3. Fall in love with the process.
4. Assemble your team.

When you come to the end of your own strength, your own willpower, and your own desire, don't panic. Remember how Paul confesses his inconsistency and says, "I don't really understand myself." Later in that same passage he asks a gut-wrenching question: "Oh, what a miserable person I am! Who will free me from this life that is dominated by sin and death?" (Rom. 7:15, 24 NLT).

His answer? "Thank God! The answer is in Jesus Christ our Lord" (Rom. 7:25 NLT).

So we pre-decide to be consistent, with God's help.

- "With God's help, I will not drink soda."
- "With God's help, I will walk three times a week."
- "With God's help, I will put an extra fifty dollars a month toward paying off my credit cards."
- "With God's help, I will read the Bible daily."

- "With God's help, I will pray with my wife even if she does weird breathing stuff beforehand and prays forever and my kid starts yelling from the bathroom about explosive diarrhea."

We have to make the decision, but to keep consistent we rely on "his incomparably great power for us who believe. That power is the same as the mighty strength he exerted when he raised Christ from the dead" (Eph. 1:19–20).

In what area of your life is God calling you to be consistent? If you're not sure, take a quiet moment to pray, "God, where do you want me to be consistent? Please, show me."

Whatever it is, you can do it, with God's help.

PART 6 EXERCISES

1. On a scale of 1 to 10, how would you rate yourself on consistency today? Explain your score.
2. List at least three areas in your life where you feel you are consistent.
3. List at least three areas in your life where you feel you are inconsistent.
4. Looking at your answers to questions 2 and 3, what do you think are the major factors that make the difference between the lists?
5. Have you ever blamed genetics, background, appearance, intelligence, or education as an excuse for an inconsistency? Explain.
6. Is there something in your life that you want to be great at, but inconsistency has been your biggest obstacle? Explain.
7. Write down your greatest unfulfilled goal. That's the *what*. Next, write down your best *why*.
8. Review the three areas of inconsistency you wrote down, and write a strong why for each one.
9. Do you have any perfectionistic tendencies? How does your answer affect your decision-making—positively or negatively?
10. In what areas of your life do you need to let go of the illusion of perfectionism? Be specific.
11. Is there any area in your life where not planning to fail is keeping you from being consistent? Explain.
12. Consider creating a support team. Write down anyone who comes to mind who might be part of your "two or three."
13. How might adding "with God's help" be a game changer in your inconsistent areas?
14. How can you practically apply that truth to each inconsistency you listed?

PART 7

I Will Be a Finisher

Now finish the work, so that your eager willingness to do it may be matched by your completion of it, according to your means.

—2 CORINTHIANS 8:11

Voting on Your Future

In high school I played several sports, but my best was tennis. I drew the interest of a college team, who sent a recruiter to see me play in the state championship tournament. He sat in the stands watching me compete in the semifinal match against a top-ranked, undefeated opponent. I played the match of my life and beat him 6–3, 6–2. (I say "beat," but the more accurate way to describe it is "wiped the court with his undefeated butt." Yes, I'm bragging. But remember, pride comes before a fall.)

The scout came over and signed me on the spot.

He left, and I went on to play in the finals against a guy I had defeated two weeks earlier, but he beat me. (I say "beat," but the more accurate way to describe it is "waxed the court with my overconfident butt.") It's safe to say that if the recruiter had watched my last match, I would never have gotten the chance to play for this top-ranked NAIA school. I was about to learn I was significantly outclassed.

Soon I was off to college with my tennis scholarship. On my first day there I played a practice match against one of my teammates—and lost 6–0, 6–0. (Waxed again.) I didn't win a game. Not a single one. It's impossible to adequately describe how embarrassed and humiliated I felt. It was painfully obvious to everyone that I had no business playing for a team of this caliber.

I wasn't a Christian yet, and I was not very Christian-y. I screamed. I cussed. I slammed my racket. Then I slammed my backup racket and stormed off the court in shame.

One of the guys on our team knew my high school coach and called to let him know what happened.

Two hours later I was sitting in my dorm room, still steaming, employing my full arsenal of profanity, committed to quitting the team. I wasn't anywhere close to good enough, and I couldn't face the shame of being outclassed. That's when there was a knock on my dorm room door. My high school coach, Coach Ellinger, had driven an hour and a half and was standing there.

He walked in, sat down across from me on my roommate's bed, and said, "So this is the kind of person you are, huh? I never saw you as a quitter."

I told him to go some places and to do some things. (Remember, this was before I was a Christian, and I still had an unsanctified vocabulary.)

I was furious at the world, but his shockingly generous gesture gave me pause. *My former coach dropped everything to drive one hundred miles to my dorm room to talk to me.* The gravity of the moment set in. Somehow, I sensed there was more at stake in this whole situation than just a tennis match.

My coach gathered himself and spoke to me almost prophetically. He said words I would never forget. "Craig, this is a big day in your life. I'm glad I'm here to get to see it. Today you are gonna determine what kind of person you are. Are you like most people? Will you give up when things get tough? Or will you finish what you started? Do you quit in the face of adversity? Or will you overcome?"

His question hung in the air for what seemed like eternity.

So I ask you, What kind of person are you going to be?

You may not have broken all of your tennis rackets or cursed at your coach in your dorm room, but you've probably contemplated quitting something important. You may feel like giving up right now.

- You had a dream and pursued your goal with gusto but hit some resistance and your effort stalled out. You've had little to no progress. Frustration has set in. You're discouraged. You feel like giving up.
- There was a relationship you tried to restore. You reached out to initiate healing, but it didn't go well. Things are worse today than they were before.

- You may be working to save your marriage, but your spouse isn't cooperating, and you are running out of fight.
- You've been praying and praying for your child to come back to Jesus, or for healing, or for financial provision, or for God to help you overcome an addiction, but your prayers aren't getting the results you want, and you are almost out of hope.
- You've battled a debilitating depression, and the pain simply won't subside. You don't want to give up on life, but you wonder how much longer you'll have the strength to go on.

I've talked to people who want to give up, and they'll say, "Craig, I'm done." You might feel that way. If so, let me remind you:

If you're not dead, you're not done. God has more for you.

I understand that you're discouraged and feel like giving up, but God has more for you to do:

- more love to give
- more people to help
- more ministries to start
- more businesses to launch
- more content to create
- more hope to share
- more friendships to make

You may feel too tired to get excited about "more." You might be thinking, *More? I'm so tired. I can't do more.*

If that's true, consider what David Allen says in his book *Getting Things Done*: "Much of the stress that people feel doesn't come from having too much to do. It comes from not finishing what they've started."[45]

Could the issue be not that you have too much to do but that you haven't yet done what God's called you to do?

Do you have some unfinished business?

Please pause to reflect on this question: What has God prompted you to do that you haven't done yet?

Perhaps you'd be wise to take the advice Paul gave to the Corinthians: "It would be good for you to finish what you started" (2 Cor. 8:10 NLT).

Why does this matter so much?

If you have regrets because of things you've quit on in the past, or if you're agonizing about giving up on something that really matters, you know why this is a big deal. You don't want to feel that way anymore.

But it goes even deeper, because this is not just about now, it's about the rest of your life. What you do now determines who you become. Why?

> Every decision you make is a vote on your future.

Today's decisions are votes on what kind of person you will be tomorrow. Anytime you quit, you vote on becoming a person who doesn't have what it takes and doesn't finish what they start.

But every time you are strong in the Lord and persevere, you cast a vote that you will be a finisher.

Which brings me back to my dorm room.

Remember my coach said, "I never saw you as a quitter. Today, you're gonna determine what kind of person you are." Then he asked, "Who are you, Craig? Will you give up when things get tough? Or will you finish what you started? Do you quit in the face of adversity? Or will you overcome?"

His questions pulled me out of my immediate situation and forced me to think ahead. I knew the answer right away. I knew who I wanted to be. In that moment I pre-decided:

> When I commit, I do not quit.

It's impossible to describe what that moment meant to me. That decision to persevere was so much bigger than tennis. It was about character. It was about mindset. It was about commitment. In every area of life, I'd be a person who finishes what he starts.

I went back to tennis and worked hard to persevere. I was the first to practice and the last to leave. On off days, I still trained hard. With so much ground to make up, I determined no one would outwork me on the court.

Honestly, I barely survived my first year. (Being the lone American on an all-international team, I had the only car to drive my teammates to practice. I'm pretty sure the sole reason I didn't get cut is because I was the transportation.) I got a little better my second year. I was undefeated my third year. In my fourth year I won the athlete of the year award for my entire college.

Is that because I was a superior athlete?

No.

It's because I didn't quit.

With God's help, I've taken that same attitude into everything.

> You may see me struggle, but you won't see me quit.

When I commit, I do not quit. I am a finisher.

What kind of person will you be? The decisions you make today are votes toward who you will become tomorrow.

Before you start, decide you won't quit. It's time to pre-decide today:

> I will be a finisher.

Are you ready to make that decision?

When you do, you will go farther, because this is a key factor—perhaps *the* key factor—in pleasing God, accomplishing our goals, and achieving success.

7.2

True Grit

What separates people with average achievements from those who accomplish amazing things? What's the difference between those who maximize their potential and those who always seem to struggle and underperform? It's not their talent or intelligence or who they know. It's perseverance.

Perseverance is the path to greatness.

Angela Duckworth is a brilliant scholar—she went to Harvard and Oxford—and has spent years studying why successful people succeed. She's examined the lives of

- people who survived and thrived at West Point military academy,
- poor kids in rough inner-city schools and rich kids in Ivy League colleges,
- businesspeople who have made millions,
- and kids who make the finals of the Scripps National Spelling Bee.

So why do successful people succeed?
Grit.
That's what she's found. Grit. Grit is a strength of character that refuses to quit. Grit is perseverance even in the face of adversity.
Duckworth says:

"Enthusiasm is common. Endurance is rare."

She explains that people who are successful set a goal and are willing to give up lesser goals. Every morning they get up, point themselves in the direction of their goal, and take a step toward it. They don't hope to accomplish it. They don't daydream about it. They focus their reality on achieving the goal.[46]

Successful people succeed because of grit.

That's really good news for you and me. It means

- it's okay if you're not the most talented,
- it's not a problem if you don't know the right people,
- it's not the end of the world if you're not especially educated.

It means you can overcome, achieve your goals, and live an amazing, God-honoring life if you just keep putting one foot in front of the other.

That's why we're going to pre-decide. I am a finisher:

When I commit, I do not quit.

Because what separates average from amazing is grit.

We see this in every arena of life.

In politics, I think of Nelson Mandela, who became the president of South Africa and inspired unprecedented change in his nation after being imprisoned for twenty-seven years.

In music, U2 is one of the most successful bands ever, having won twenty-two Grammy Awards, more than any other band. They've sold more than 150 million records, and in 2005 they were inducted into the Rock & Roll Hall of Fame. Was it easy for them because of their enormous talent? No. U2 did so poorly starting out that they had to survive on twenty-five pounds a week, provided by their manager, Paul McGuinness. Bus fares for the band had to be scrounged from a jar of coins on McGuinness's desk.[47] It was not easy for U2. They could have given up, like so many bands do, but they had grit.

Regardless of how anyone may feel about him now, Will Smith is the only actor to have starred in eight consecutive films that grossed more than $100 million at the US box office. He's been nominated for five Golden Globes and two Academy Awards, and he has won four Grammy Awards. Why has Will been so successful? Natural acting ability? Nope. Here's his explanation: "The only thing that I see that is distinctly different about me is I'm not afraid to die on a treadmill. I will not be outworked, period. You might have more talent than me, you might be smarter than me, you might be sexier than me, you might be all of those things, you got it on me in nine categories. But if we get on the treadmill together, there's two things: you're getting off first, or I'm going to die. It's really that simple, right?"[48]

And who is the most successful business leader of our generation? It's debatable, but many would argue Steve Jobs. Did he have an easy path? No. His birth mother gave him up for adoption. He was suspended from school several times and dropped out of college. He founded Apple, then got *fired* from Apple. He had to fight for twelve years to take back the company he started. It would have been easy to give up, but he chose to persevere.

We see this in every arena of life, including the kingdom of God. Study the lives of people who have had incredible impact for God—John Wesley, William Carey, Mother Teresa, Charles Spurgeon, Harriet Tubman, Martin Luther King Jr., and on and on—and you'll see that they went years without any results but overcame overwhelming obstacles by refusing to quit. They gave up lesser goals for the ultimate goal God gave them. They got up every morning, pointed themselves in the direction of their goal, and took another step. No matter what happened, they refused to quit.

Grit led them to greatness.

The apostle Paul is a perfect example. Late in his life we find him in prison where he is awaiting execution. From that jail cell Paul writes an emotional letter to Timothy, his spiritual son and ministry apprentice. Paul encourages Timothy to be strong: "You then, my child, be strengthened by the grace that is in Christ Jesus" (2 Tim. 2:1 ESV).

Paul tells Timothy to expect suffering but to overcome it and be a finisher: "But you should keep a clear mind in every situation. Don't be afraid of suffering for the Lord. Work at telling others the Good News, and fully carry out the ministry God has given you" (2 Tim. 4:5 NLT).

He's encouraging Timothy to persevere. Why? Because Paul knew what he himself had been through. Paul had suffered rejection, betrayal, persecution, physical beatings, stoning, and imprisonment. He knew Timothy would experience similar things, so he told him, "It's going to be hard, but don't you quit. Others will, but not you, Timothy."

Paul could say that because he hadn't quit and had accomplished the goal. Check out what he writes next: "As for me, my life has already been poured out as an offering to God. The time of my death is near. I have fought the good fight, I have finished the race, and I have remained faithful. And now the prize awaits me—the crown of righteousness, which the Lord, the righteous Judge, will give me on the day of his return" (2 Tim. 4:6–8 NLT).

How cool is it that Paul could write that as he faced death? He basically says, "I pre-decided I am faithful and I am an influencer and here I am at the end and I did it." Years earlier he had shared decisions he had made about his life: "However, I consider my life worth nothing to me; my only aim is to finish the race and complete the task the Lord Jesus has given me—the task of testifying to the good news of God's grace" (Acts 20:24).

Now he is at the end of his race, and he tells Timothy, "I did it. I did what God gave me to do. I am a finisher."

I'm sure Paul would encourage you in the same way he did Timothy. It's going to be difficult. You will suffer along the way, but don't give up. You are a finisher. When you commit, you don't quit. Or as he wrote in another letter, "So let's not get tired of doing what is good. At just the right time we will reap a harvest of blessing if we don't give up" (Gal. 6:9 NLT).

We need to not get tired, to not give up, to achieve greatness through perseverance, to be finishers, to pre-decide:

> When I commit, I do not quit.

We need to grow in grit.

We'll talk about how to do that, but first let's address the question of why people quit.

7.3

Quitting

Can you name people who have quit?

Yes. Tons.

We can all think of people who have quit on their dreams, diets, marriages, God, careers, or recovery from addiction. That's not even to mention how many have quit taking piano lessons or eating brussels sprouts.

If perseverance is the path to greatness, why do so many give up? No one starts with the idea of quitting, so why might we end up doing it?

The Option

Remember the movie *Apollo 13*? NASA is trying to get the Apollo spacecraft and the three astronauts safely back to Earth after an oxygen tank in the service module failed two days into the mission. The chance of success looks bad, even impossible. At one point a NASA official lists all of the problems to another, who responds, "This could be the worst disaster NASA's ever experienced." But flight director Gene Kranz interrupts: "With all due respect, sir, I believe this is going to be our finest hour." Later he announces to his team, "Failure is not an option!"[49]

One reason people quit is because they give themselves the option of quitting. Perhaps that is part of the reason why about half of marriages end in divorce. If we studied those marriages, we would find all kinds of reasons why, but one thing they all have in common is that at least one person in each couple allowed for the possibility of divorce. Couples who don't consider divorce an option fight through the difficulties and figure out how to make their marriages work. Couples who consider it an option are more likely to bail when the difficulties seem unbearable.

It's not just marriage. You've probably gone on a diet and lasted only a week. But perhaps you've had other goals that were so important you never allowed failure to enter your mind.

People quit because they give themselves the option of quitting.

To be clear, I'm not saying you should never quit. I give you permission to quit quilting, quibbling, and perhaps anything else that starts with a Q. There are times you should strategically quit something.

- You might want to quit one job to take one with better hours so you can spend more time with your children.
- You might quit your major in school to pursue something more meaningful to you.
- Perhaps you are in a dead-end dating relationship that is distracting you from pursuing Jesus. You'd probably be wise to quit that relationship and trust God for something better.

When I say you don't quit, I'm not suggesting you be bullheaded or unwise. I'm hopeful you'll live with selective grit. "Let your eyes look straight ahead; fix your gaze directly before you. Give careful thought to the paths for your feet and be steadfast in all your ways. Do not turn to the right or the left" (Prov. 4:25–27).

When God calls you, when you know it's important, you don't quit. It's not an option.

Seeing through the Fog

Florence Chadwick became famous for being the first woman to swim the English Channel—both ways. She then set another swimming goal. On July 4, 1952, she started her swim from Catalina Island to the California coastline. Unfortunately, she didn't quite make it.

What stopped her?

It wasn't cold water, or sharks, or exhaustion from the sixteen-hour swim.

What stopped her was fog.

Fog rolled in, and Chadwick could no longer see the coastline, so she quit.

When she climbed into the boat after sixteen hours of swimming, she discovered she was less than a mile from her goal. (Nooooooo!) She later told reporters she would have made it if she could have seen land.

Two months later she made a second attempt. Again, fog set in, but this time she made it. Why? She said she expected the fog and kept a mental image of the shoreline in her mind the entire time she swam.[50]

Why will we be tempted to quit?

Because we can't see the future.

We have a goal, but so often it doesn't seem within reach. But that's okay. Why?

- We embrace boring. We consider it a win every day we show up.
- We move forward with why-power. Remember, we start with why and keep our why fixed before us. We know what we're fighting for.
- We know reward is coming. "At just the right time we will reap a harvest of blessing if we don't give up" (Gal. 6:9 NLT). People who persevere look forward to the rewards of greatness. They see what cannot be seen.

After Peter denied Jesus three times and realized his guilt, the news of Judas's choice to end his own life was probably still fresh. The only reason Peter was able to have the risen Lord assign him to "feed my sheep" in John 21 was because, between the trials and the tomb, he didn't quit. Peter didn't let his guilt overpower him and give up. Jesus had become enough of Peter's why for him to see the shore through the fog.

The Hard Way

Why do people quit?

Because it's hard. (#DUH)

What's hard? *It* is.

If it is something that will help us grow or will improve a relationship or increase our impact in the world, it will be hard. If you decide to

- go on a mission trip, the money you need to raise likely won't come in as quickly as you thought it would;
- lose weight and get in shape, people are going to keep bringing doughnuts in to work;
- improve your marriage by going to counseling, your spouse may not want to go;
- go back to college while still working full-time, it will likely be tougher than you imagined;
- volunteer at church on Sunday mornings, something will often go wrong that makes it almost impossible to get there on time;
- get out of debt and live on a budget, it won't be long before your car breaks down and you won't have enough money for the repairs;
- stop cursing, you can count on stepping on one of your kid's Legos.

When that happens, don't be surprised. It's always hard.

Jesus promised it would be hard: "In this world you will have trouble" (John 16:33).

It's hard, so what do we do? "Let us throw off everything that hinders and the sin that so easily entangles. And let us run with perseverance the race marked out for us" (Heb. 12:1). How? "We do this by keeping our eyes on Jesus, the champion who initiates and perfects our faith" (Heb. 12:2 NLT).

Want to hear something fascinating? Those verses were originally written in Greek, and the word translated "race" in English is *agona*. *Agona* is where we get our word "agony." So basically we're told, "Let us run with perseverance the agony marked out for us."

It's always hard but it's always worth it. Remember your why! That's what Jesus did. The next sentence in Hebrews says, "For the joy set before him he endured the cross" (Heb. 12:2). He endured the agony because of the joy that was coming.

It's always hard, but it's always hard for *everyone*. You're not alone. And those who persevere stop feeling sorry for themselves and learn to embrace the difficulties.

Have you heard about Erik Weihenmayer? At the age of fourteen, he went blind. Well, *that* is when you start feeling sorry for yourself and decide to quit, right? Not Erik. He went on to be a champion wrestler in high school. He then climbed the seven summits—the highest points on every continent. He's one of only 150 people to have ever done that. And he did it blind![51]

It might surprise you that someone with such a significant disability could accomplish such an incredible feat.

It shouldn't.

It's often the people who have faced the most difficulty who succeed the most wildly.

For instance, did you know that 67 percent of British prime ministers from the beginning of the nineteenth century to World War II and almost a third of all US presidents lost a parent when they were children?[52] And did you know that about a third of successful entrepreneurs are dyslexic?[53]

In his book *David and Goliath: Underdogs, Misfits, and the Art of Battling Giants*, Malcolm Gladwell shares those statistics, and stories of multitudes of people who chose to overcome. He writes about what he calls "desirable difficulties," explaining that having to face horrible circumstances is actually an opportunity rather than an obstacle.[54] Why? It forces people to grow in grit. (These stats make me feel better about getting rejected for ordination. And they might make you feel better if you have a significant obstacle you believe is holding you back.)

Gladwell suggests that those who have overcome disability or disadvantage succeed not in spite of their circumstances but because of them.

You can too. It will be hard, but God is for you. And according to Romans 8:37, in all of the opposition you face, you are more than a conqueror through God who loves you.

That's the key to not quitting—through God who loves us. We persevere "by keeping our eyes on Jesus" (Heb. 12:2 NLT).

7.4

Take Another Step

My wife, Amy, was sitting by me at a conference when, out of the blue, she leaned over and whispered solemnly, "God wants me to start transition homes for abused women." You may think that a pastor's wife talks like that all the time. No. Certainly not this pastor's wife. There are two things that stood out about her declaration. First, she'd never once said God wanted her to start something. Second, I've never seen her more confident of anything in her life.

God wanted her to start a transition home for abused women.

Knowing God had sparked a vision, Amy set out to do his will. After researching, studying, and seeking wisdom, Amy had a clear understanding of the general location, size, type, and price needed for the first home to start this ministry. The only problem was that she couldn't find any that would work.

God was guiding. But he didn't seem to be providing.

Amy searched. And searched. And searched. After months of letdowns and dead ends, she crashed hard into an emotional wall. Her confidence collapsed and she said, through tears, "Maybe I didn't hear from God after all. Maybe I should just quit."

You may feel now the way Amy felt then. You might be on the edge of giving up and walking away from a dream. When you're tempted to quit, try to remember who your life is for.

For God

You are a finisher. *When I commit, I do not quit.* You have a race to run, and you will finish.

Remember what Paul said? "However, I consider my life worth

nothing to me; my only aim is to finish the race and complete the task the Lord Jesus has given me—the task of testifying to the good news of God's grace" (Acts 20:24).

At the end of his life, Paul told Timothy he did it, he finished the race. How?

He wasn't running for himself. He said, "I consider my life worth nothing to me." He was proclaiming *It's not about me. It's not about my desires. It's not about my dreams. It's not about my future. It's not about my popularity.*

I consider my life worth nothing to me.

If you're tempted to quit what God's called you to start, it may be because you care about something more than you care about God and running the race he's set before you.

We're all tempted to put something ahead of God and his will for our lives. What is that thing for you? You may want to acknowledge it and declare that it's not going to stop you anymore. Make Paul's statement your own:

However, I consider my _____ worth nothing to me; my only aim is to finish the race and complete the task the Lord Jesus has given me.

What goes in that blank for you?

- I consider my <u>personal comfort</u> worth nothing to me.
- I consider the <u>opinions of other people</u> worth nothing to me.
- I consider my <u>social media follows</u> worth nothing to me.
- I consider my <u>net worth</u> worth nothing to me.
- I consider my <u>personal dreams</u> worth nothing to me.

My only aim is to finish the race and complete the task the Lord Jesus has given me.

We commit to him, and we don't quit. We are finishers. We run our race for God.

When we grow weary, we remember who we're running for and we take the next step. You don't have to finish the race today. You just need to take one more step.

Remember what Angela Duckworth found? Gritty people who overcome get up, point themselves in the direction of their goal, and take one more step.

You just need to get up and fight one more round. On September 7, 1892, a boxer named "Gentleman Jim" Corbett entered the ring to fight arguably the greatest boxer of all time, John L. Sullivan. Sullivan was the last heavyweight champion of bare-knuckle boxing and the first heavyweight champion of gloved boxing. When he got in the ring that day, he was 50–0.

Sullivan lost only one fight in his entire career. That one.

Gentleman Jim Corbett had a mantra he lived by in the ring: "Fight one more round."

He didn't think of himself as the most talented or best. But he would never quit.

He got knocked around by John Sullivan that day. But he wouldn't stay down. *Fight one more round.*

Back then the fight kept going until someone couldn't fight anymore. There could be a lot of rounds. This match went twenty-one rounds. That's when Gentleman Jim finally knocked out John Sullivan and became the heavyweight champion of the world.[55]

You may get knocked down. We all get knocked down. But you get up, and you fight one more round. You take one more step.

What about Amy and her vision to start transition homes for abused women? That's what she did as well. When everything in her felt it was time to quit, she took another step.

After countless potential homes didn't make the cut, she made another call. That's when she heard about the "perfect house." When I say perfect, except for the price (which was way out of our range), it was as perfect as any house could be, almost as if it had been designed as a ministry home.

When we stepped into the newly remodeled home, we met the seller. With unbridled passion, Janet explained that she bought the house to flip it. But midway through her construction, she believed God called her to also furnish the home. (*What? That makes no sense.*) Prompted by God, she installed a commercial-grade kitchen, transformed extra rooms into bedrooms, and furnished it with twin beds and bunk beds in several rooms. This four-bedroom house could comfortably sleep eight women, with space for group dining and large group gatherings. It also had private quarters for a house director. That's when the bizarre story got even crazier.

Janet cried as she described the process. "I had planned to flip the house for a sizable profit. But I just couldn't shake the feeling that this home was supposed to be used to help hurting women."

By this point we were all crying.

Then lightning struck. She told us, "I think I'm supposed to donate the house, furniture, and all, to be your first transitional home."

God had indeed guided. And God, in his perfect timing, had provided. Why? Because Amy didn't quit.

Now Branch15 has multiple homes in cities across Oklahoma helping women escape human trafficking, drug addiction, and physical abuse, and transition out of incarceration back into healthy living.

Just take another step.

Who is the perfect example? Jesus.

Day by day, he took the next step. Look at his final words on the cross: "Jesus said, 'It is finished.' With that, he bowed his head and gave up his spirit" (John 19:30).

As Paul would say, and as I hope to say, Jesus was telling his Father, "I did everything you sent me to do. I finished the race."

How did he do it? He wasn't running for himself. He was running for his Father. And day after day, week after week, month after month, year after year, painful moment after painful moment, he just took the next step.

- When they hated him, he took the next step and loved them back.
- When they struck him, he took the next step and turned the other cheek.
- When he was carrying the cross up the hill and fell to the ground, he took the next step by getting back up.
- When they nailed him to the cross, and then mocked him, he took the next step and said, "Father, forgive them, for they do not know what they are doing" (Luke 23:34).

- When he had defeated sin and death and hell, he took the next step, out of the tomb.

From the beginning, he had pre-decided: *I am ready, devoted, faithful, influential, generous, and consistent, and when I commit, I don't quit, because I am a finisher.*

So what are *you* going to do? Every time you get knocked down, whenever you're tempted to give up, you decide to take another step.

- Say one more prayer.
- Make one more call.
- Give one more gift.
- Forgive one more time.
- Run one more mile.
- Ask for one more meeting.
- Memorize one more verse.
- Attend one more session with your counselor.
- Make it through one more day of sobriety.
- Have one more gracious conversation with your teenager.
- Continue to dream that dream.
- Don't give up.

You take another step because you are not running for yourself. You're running for God.

But what about when you get tired and feel like you can't take another step? When you've given, but they didn't care? When you've prayed, but with no results? When you've loved but been taken advantage of? What do you do when you feel like you can't run anymore?

That's when you remember that you're running *with* God.

With God

In the 1992 Summer Olympics in Barcelona there was a British runner named Derek Redmond, who was one of the favorites in the 400-meter race. He got off to a great start but midway through the race ruptured his hamstring and fell to the ground in excruciating pain.

His dreams were crushed. Years of training, sacrifice, and single-minded devotion vanished instantly. Not willing to give up, but in agonizing pain, Derek attempted to stand up and hobble toward the finish line. Then, in one of the most emotional moments in sports history, his dad ran down from the stands, climbed over the railing, and ran to the track. He told his injured son, "We're going to finish this together," and basically carried him to the finish line.[56]

You have a heavenly Father who loves you and is always by your side. He assures you, "I have made you and I will carry you" (Isa. 46:4). You never run alone. And so you can be "confident of this, that he who began a good work in you will carry it on to completion until the day of Christ Jesus" (Phil. 1:6).

When you are tired, disappointed, and weary, you don't quit, you cry out to God.

God, I don't understand. I don't get it. But I am trying to trust you. I am clinging to you, God. I'm holding on. I won't let you go, and I will not quit.

When you're struggling, think about God and remember what God thinks about you. Remember Hebrews 12:2 from earlier? "For the joy set before him he endured the cross." No matter how many times you may have read that verse before, have you ever thought about what that joy was? It was you. Jesus went to the cross for you. You were the reward he received for running his race and enduring the cross.

He fixed his eyes on us. Now we fix our eyes on him.

He ran his race. Now we're running ours. And we "run with perseverance the race marked out for us" (Heb. 12:1) by "keeping our eyes on Jesus, the champion who initiates and perfects our faith" (Heb. 12:2 NLT).

How will that help?

• When we fix our eyes on Jesus, we strengthen our hearts. "Consider him who endured such opposition from sinners, so that you will not grow weary and lose heart" (Heb. 12:3).

- When we fix our eyes on Jesus, we put our confidence in God instead of ourselves.

    "Such confidence we have through Christ before God. Not that we are competent in ourselves to claim anything for ourselves, but our competence comes from God" (2 Cor. 3:4–5).
- When we fix our eyes on Jesus, we have confidence because we know we can do all things through his strength, and that our confidence will be rewarded.

    "So do not throw away your confidence; it will be richly rewarded. You need to persevere so that when you have done the will of God, you will receive what he has promised" (Heb. 10:35–36).

You are running for God and with God.

You never run alone.

God loves you and will carry you.

So fix your eyes on Jesus. He is a finisher, and so are you.

When I commit, I do not quit.

PART 7 EXERCISES

1. What do you believe has been the biggest finish in your life so far?
2. What do you believe is the biggest unfinished goal in your life?
3. Have you ever had a crossroads moment like I had with tennis in college? Did anyone intervene for you like my coach did with me?
4. Is there something you are tempted to quit right now? Explain.
5. Take some time to prayerfully answer the questions I offered in this section: Do you have some unfinished business? What has God prompted you to do that you haven't done yet?
6. Personalize this sentence: You may see me struggle with _____, but I promise you won't see me quit.
7. What is the one thing that, at the end of your life, you want to be able to look back and say, "I did it!"
8. Is there anything you have been thinking of quitting for which you need to take the option of quitting off the table? Explain.
9. Is there anything you have refused to quit, but that you need to get out of your life for your own well-being? Explain.
10. Is there an area of your life where you are refusing to quit, but difficulties and disadvantages keep opposing you? Explain.
11. What might be the one thing you need to acknowledge and declare won't stop you anymore? What goes in that blank for you, using Paul's statement in Acts 20:24 as your own? "I consider my _____ worth nothing to me; my only aim is to finish the race and complete the task the Lord Jesus has given me."
12. How can my wife's story with the transitional home give you hope and encouragement to take your next step toward what you are called to finish?
13. How might accepting the truth that you are running with God change your perspective on finishing?
14. Rewrite in your own words: God, I am committed to _____ so I will fix my eyes on you and be a finisher.

Conclusion
Pre-Choose This Day

Amazeballs

What do you want to be amazing at?

Seriously, think about it. If you could choose just one thing, what would it be?

I'll share mine in a moment, but first I've got to tell you about Kobe.

Kobe Bryant was amazeballs at basketball.

Of the more than one hundred billion people who have ever lived and the nearly five thousand people who have played professionally in the NBA, Kobe is regularly ranked in the top five to ten ever to have hooped.

Why was Kobe so crazy good?

He said it was the power of pre-decision.

Kobe talked about growing up in Italy with a love for basketball but moving to the United States and realizing he was way behind the other kids his age.[57] He could not compete but was not about to give up on basketball. He committed to growing his game, skill by skill, over the long haul. Each year he would pre-decide one improvement to focus on.

In high school he would practice in the gym, by himself, from 5:00 to 7:00 a.m. before school.

He emphasized the need to work consistently, being patient as he gradually caught up to and then surpassed the other players. He said his plan looked like this: Monday—get better. Tuesday—get better. Wednesday—get better. Do that over three, four, five, ten years and "you will get where you need to go."[58] He said that "the results don't really matter" because it was all about falling in love with the process.[59]

You might assume that was just when he was in high school, trying to catch up to the other players. No. Kobe made so much progress that he shot to the NBA straight from high school. And even while in the pros, he continued to pre-decide his personal workouts and which skills he would focus on improving, outworking everyone else.

Former Lakers head coach Byron Scott said he would find Kobe practicing, by himself, in a dark gym two hours before practice. He watched Kobe from the shadows and determined, "This kid is gonna be great."[60]

Former Lakers teammate John Celestand shared that Kobe was always the first player in the gym, even when he was injured and couldn't play.[61]

Kobe played on the US Olympic team, and one of the trainers described how he once held a personal workout from 4:15 a.m. to 11:00 a.m., refusing to leave the gym until he made eight hundred shots.[62]

Asked how he wanted to be remembered, Kobe said, "To think of me as a person that's overachieved, that would mean a lot to me. That means I put a lot of work in and squeezed every ounce of juice out of this orange that I could."[63]

What made Kobe, Kobe? I would tell you pre-decisions. He called them "contracts." Each year he made a contract with himself for what he would do to take his game to the next level. During his NBA career, he made a contract with himself each summer for his off-season workout plan.

He admitted that, after pre-deciding, he would face constant inner challenges. An inner whisper would tell him to back off. That he was doing too much. That his knee was really sore, so he needed to take just one day off.

But Kobe never listened to those voices. He explained, "I'm not negotiating with myself. The deal was already made. Beginning of summer. I signed that contract with myself and I'm doing it."[64]

I am ridiculously inspired by the way Kobe would think ahead, by his pre-decisions. It's what empowered him to be one of basketball's all-time greats.

The power of pre-decision is what puts people on the path of success.

It's cool that Kobe used it with basketball—but me?

I want to be amazing at life.

I want to be amazing at living my life for God.

35,000

35,000.

We began our journey together with that number: 35,000. It's the number of decisions we make on an average day.

I am still overwhelmed by that number. It makes me tired. Knowing tomorrow you will wake up and have to make 35,000 decisions might make you not want to get up tomorrow.

But there's good news: seven.

We've learned seven essential pre-decisions that will automatize many of the more important of those 35,000 decisions and will set us on a path to the abundant life Jesus offers.

It reminds me of the choice Moses set before the Israelites before he died.

Bahar

Moses knows this is his last chance to speak to the Israelites, the people he led and shepherded for decades. Of every talk he's ever given, this speech is his last and most important. This is it, and Moses doesn't pull any punches. "Now listen! Today I am giving you a choice between life and death, between prosperity and disaster" (Deut. 30:15 NLT).

He implores them: "Oh, that you would choose life, so that you and your descendants might live! You can make this choice by loving the LORD your God, obeying him, and committing yourself firmly to him. This is the key to your life" (Deut. 30:19–20 NLT).

To us, "choose" feels like "you have options and get to pick one," but the Hebrew word Moses spoke, translated "choose" in English, is pregnant with deeper meaning. The Hebrew word is *bahar*, and it is almost always used in the Bible with theological significance.[65] The word expresses that this choice has foundational and eternal significance.[66]

Interestingly, the word is typically used to describe God choosing us, signifying that this is a person (or, in the case of the Israelites, a nation) God has chosen as his own.[67]

Here are some examples:

- "For the LORD has chosen Jacob to be his own, Israel to be his treasured possession" (Ps. 135:4).
- "He chose the tribe of Judah, Mount Zion, which he loved" (Ps. 78:68).
- "I have chosen David to rule my people Israel" (1 Kings 8:16).
- "He has chosen my son Solomon to sit on the throne of the kingdom of the LORD over Israel" (1 Chron. 28:5).
- "David said to Michal, 'It was before the LORD, who chose me'" (2 Sam. 6:21).

Do you see it?

God chose us. Now he's asking us if we'll choose him.

Moses is about to die. There's no time for playing games. So he asks the Israelites: Will you choose God? It's the path of life. You don't have to, but if you don't, you will put yourself on the path of death.

Moses delivers his last speech, passes away, and Joshua takes over leadership of the Israelites. He leads them into the promised land and into several battles. Soon Joshua is at the end of his life and, like Moses before him, declares his last words to the Israelites. This is it, and Joshua doesn't pull any punches either: "Choose this day whom you will serve, whether the gods your fathers served in the region beyond the River, or the gods of the Amorites in whose land you dwell. But as for me and my house, we will serve the LORD" (Josh. 24:15 ESV).

Like Moses, Joshua wants to talk about *bahar*. Why? Because what really matters is our choices. Every decision matters, but there are a few that are foundational and possess eternal significance. The main one is this:

Will you choose God?

He has chosen you. Will you choose him?

Joshua tells the Israelites the choice is up to them, but as for Joshua and his family? They had pre-decided: We choose God.

Seven

Seven.

We began our journey together with two numbers: 35,000 and seven.

I have proposed seven pre-decisions that will allow you to take your life back and put you on the path of life. Why are these decisions essential? Because when you make them, as Moses said, you are "committing yourself firmly to him. This is the key to your life" (Deut. 30:20 NLT).

At the beginning of this book, I asked if you were ready to make the seven life-defining pre-decisions. Now that you've learned why they are each so vital, it's time to determine your life direction.

Moses prepared his last speech and didn't hold back. In the same way, Joshua brought fire from heaven and challenged God's people to make a choice.

Although I'm certainly no Moses or Joshua, these are my final words to you in this book. And because of what's at stake, I won't hold back.

Are you sick and tired of losing battles to the devil, giving in to temptation, and regretting sinning against God?

Are you done living with good spiritual intentions, but not following through?

Do you sense, deep down, that God has more for you? That he doesn't just want you to be happy, or successful? That God wants you faithful?

Do you hate being easily influenced by the people and patterns of this world? Are you ready to be salt and light, influencing others toward Jesus each day?

Are you sick of being selfish, and are you now primed to live with a heart of incredible generosity?

Do you hate being inconsistent, and instead, driven by why-power, are you now ready to do consistently what you used to do occasionally?

Will you draw a line in the sand that when you commit, you don't quit?

It's time to decide. Do you want more of what you have? Then do more of what you already do. If you want the same life you've been living, then keep on doing the same old thing you've been doing. But if you want something different, it's time to stop reacting and think ahead. It's time to make seven pre-decisions that will change your life.

Are you ready?

If so, let's do it. Let's pre-decide:

- I will be ready.
- I will be devoted.
- I will be faithful.
- I will be an influencer.
- I will be generous.
- I will be consistent.
- I will be a finisher.

One thing that hits me: Moses and Joshua asked the Israelites to choose God. That may have been a challenging choice, but think about this: they already knew God had chosen them. How moving is that? Knowing they were chosen had to help them want to choose God.

In the same way, God asks us to make these seven pre-decisions, but he pre-decided to do each for us first.

He was ready.

Jesus faced all of the temptations we do, yet never sinned. That's why he was able to go to the cross and take on our sins as an innocent sacrifice.

1. *He was ready.* Jesus was prepared and available to do whatever God had for him to do.
2. *He was devoted.* He was so devoted to you he came to earth and died for you.
3. *He was faithful.* He is and always will be faithful. "If we are faithless, he remains faithful, for he cannot disown himself" (2 Tim. 2:13).

4. *He was an influencer.* Jesus has been named the most influential person ever,[68] and I doubt you'd be reading this book if he didn't first influence your life.

5. *He was generous.* We are generous because we are made in the image of a generous God, who is so giving that he gave his one and only Son.

6. *He was consistent.* He is "the same yesterday and today and forever" (Heb. 13:8). It's his absolute consistency that allows us to fully trust him in every moment, and we want to live with that same consistency so we can become more like him.

7. *He was a finisher.* Before the creation of the world, the Holy Trinity (God the Father, God the Son, and God the Holy Spirit) planned how they would save us (Eph. 1:4–5). That decision led Jesus to strip himself of the glory of heaven and come to earth and die for us. He was tempted to opt out of the plan but refused, going to the cross, from which he declared, "It is finished" (John 19:30).

Knowing God made these seven pre-decisions for us helps us want to make them for him.

So are you ready to choose who you will become?

To live the life you want to live?

More importantly, to live the life God wants you to live?

What are you going to do?

You can do what most people do. You can wake up each day, try your ever-loving hardest to make 35,000 decisions, and hope for the best.

Or you can think ahead. You can pre-decide to honor God in the most important areas of life.

Are you ready?

The choice is yours.

With God's help, you can pre-decide.

As Joshua 24:15 says, "As for me and my household, we will serve the Lord."

CONCLUSION EXERCISES

1. How does understanding that God chose you first before he asks you to choose him affect you?
2. Considering all seven "I will" statements, what was the most difficult truth for you to process? Explain.
3. Of the seven "I will" statements, which has had the most impact for you? Explain.
4. Write out a prayer to God, asking specifically for what you need him to do, while also telling him your commitment to him.

Acknowledgments

I'd like to express my deepest gratitude to all my friends who helped make this book possible.

To Amy Groeschel, thank you for your love for Jesus and your life-long commitment to our covenant of marriage. You are my dream girl forever and you are my favorite thing about everything.

Vince Antonucci, you're my writing wingman! You are one of the fastest, smartest, and hardest-working people I know. Your heart for this project shows on every single page. Thank you for sharing your gifts with me (and others) to help reach more people. Your friendship and partnership are a gift to me. I'm forever grateful for you.

Adrianne Manning, your passion to minister to people is unpar-alleled. Thank you for caring more about our writing ministry than anyone else alive. Your heart shows in all you do and results in so many changed lives. Plus, it's a blast to work with you.

Katherine Fedor, thank you for your detailed eye. You likely cor-rected many grammatical mestake in this book (accept for the four I intentionally put in this two-sentence paragraph).

Robert Noland, your final push on the book made a massive differ-ence. Thank you for pouring your heart into the project and helping to make it stronger.

Webster Younce, Brian Phipps, Curt Diepenhorst, Katie Painter, Devin Duke, and the whole team at Zondervan, it's truly an honor to publish with you. You are mission minded in all you do, and I'm truly grateful for our publishing partnership.

Tom Winters, you are one good agent and an even better friend. Thank you for your passion to impact people through books and beyond.

To you, the reader, thank you for your trust to take this journey together. I'm praying for you as I type these final words. May God bless you with the wisdom to think ahead and make a few pre-decisions today that will create the God-honoring life he wants for you tomorrow and always!

Appendix
Takeaways and Scriptures

INTRODUCTION TAKEAWAYS

The quality of our decisions determines the quality of our lives.

As the volume of decisions increases, the quality of decisions decreases.

Decision fatigue comes when we face so many decisions
that our decision-making muscle becomes tired.

Indecision is a decision and often the enemy of progress.

These are the three enemies of excellent decisions:
1. Overwhelm
2. Fear
3. Emotion

Life is the sum of the decisions we make.

We make our decisions, and then our decisions make us.

The decisions you make today determine the stories you tell tomorrow.

Your decisions determine your direction, and
your direction determines your destiny.

You will decide now what you will do later.

Ask God to help you decide now what you will do later.

Pre-deciding reduces the number of decisions we make.

Pre-deciding reduces the fear of making the wrong decision.

Pre-deciding prevents our emotions from taking over.

When our values are clear, our decisions are easier.

These are the seven life-defining pre-decisions:
1. I will be ready.
2. I will be devoted.
3. I will be faithful.
4. I will be an influencer.
5. I will be generous.
6. I will be consistent.
7. I will be a finisher.

INTRODUCTION SCRIPTURES

I want to do what is good, but I don't. I don't want to do what is wrong, but I do it anyway.

—Romans 7:19 NLT

Forget the former things;
        do not dwell on the past.
See, I am doing a new thing!

—Isaiah 43:18–19

Commit to the LORD whatever you do,
        and he will establish your plans.

—Proverbs 16:3

But Daniel resolved not to defile himself with the royal food and wine, and he asked the chief official for permission not to defile himself this way.

—Daniel 1:8

PART 1 TAKEAWAYS

Following Jesus doesn't guarantee the absence of temptation,
it's a declaration of war against temptation.

It's not a sin to be tempted. Jesus was tempted, yet he did not sin.

Temptation typically starts with a thought.
Next comes the imagination, then justification,
until, finally, you choose to sin.

Sin thrills and then it kills. It fascinates, then it assassinates.

Sin promises satisfaction, then robs you of what you want most.
Every time you sin, you are missing out on God's best.
Choosing to sin is living a less-than life.

Most people don't plan to sin, but they still do.

God gives you the choice, rather than to fight or
give in, to pre-decide to avoid temptation.

You have a spiritual enemy, Satan, who is coming for you.
Because you matter to God, Satan wants to destroy you.

Because you are more sinful than you think you are, it makes you
less ready and therefore more vulnerable to Satan's attacks.

Your willpower will wane and wear out.

You can be ready for the moment of temptation by pre-deciding to
move the line, putting distance between you and the temptation.

Why resist a temptation tomorrow if you have
the power to eliminate it today?

The lines that God puts in your life are not
restrictive or limiting but freeing.

Satan will work to minimize the consequences,
then maximize the guilt and shame of sin.

You have to pre-decide to avoid sin by magnifying the cost.

Don't use your disappointments to justify your disobedience.

God always provides a way out of temptation, a way of escape. You can
1. move the line,
2. magnify the cost, and
3. map out the escape.

PART 1 SCRIPTURES

A prudent person foresees danger and takes precautions.
The simpleton goes blindly on and suffers the
consequences.

—Proverbs 27:12 NLT

Jesus said to him, "Away from me, Satan! For it is written:
'Worship the Lord your God, and serve him only.'"

—Matthew 4:10

For we do not have a high priest who is unable to empathize
with our weaknesses, but we have one who has been tempted in
every way, just as we are—yet he did not sin.

—Hebrews 4:15

But each person is tempted when they are dragged away by their
own evil desire and enticed. Then, after desire has conceived,
it gives birth to sin; and sin, when it is full-grown, gives birth to
death.

—James 1:14–15

Watch and pray so that you will not fall into temptation. The spirit
is willing, but the flesh is weak.

—Matthew 26:41

Be on your guard; stand firm in the faith; be courageous; be strong.
—1 Corinthians 16:13

Be alert and of sober mind. Your enemy the devil prowls around like a roaring lion looking for someone to devour.
—1 Peter 5:8

The thief comes only to steal and kill and destroy; I have come that they may have life, and have it to the full.
—John 10:10

In order that Satan might not outwit us. For we are not unaware of his schemes.
—2 Corinthians 2:11

Put on the full armor of God, so that you can take your stand against the devil's schemes.
—Ephesians 6:11

If we claim to be without sin, we deceive ourselves and the truth is not in us.
—1 John 1:8

Pride goes before destruction,
        a haughty spirit before a fall.
—Proverbs 16:18

So, if you think you are standing firm, be careful that you don't fall!
—1 Corinthians 10:12

The boundary lines have fallen for me in pleasant places;
        surely I have a delightful inheritance.
—Psalm 16:6

But if you fail to do this, you will be sinning against the LORD; and you may be sure that your sin will find you out.
—Numbers 32:23

Now Joseph was well-built and handsome, and after a while his master's wife took notice of Joseph and said, "Come to bed with me!" But he refused. . . . "How then could I do such a wicked thing and sin against God?" And though she spoke to Joseph day after day, he refused. . . . One day he went into the house to attend to his duties, and . . . she caught him by his cloak and said, "Come to bed with me!" But he left his cloak in her hand and ran out of the house.

—Genesis 39:6–12

No temptation has overtaken you except what is common to mankind. And God is faithful; he will not let you be tempted beyond what you can bear. But when you are tempted, he will also provide a way out so that you can endure it.

—1 Corinthians 10:13

Flee from sexual immorality. All other sins a person commits are outside the body, but whoever sins sexually, sins against their own body.

—1 Corinthians 6:18

Flee the evil desires of youth and pursue righteousness, faith, love and peace, along with those who call on the Lord out of a pure heart.

—2 Timothy 2:22

PART 2 TAKEAWAYS

We can't be a part-time follower of Christ.

We must continually and honestly answer the question: Am I faithfully, passionately, intentionally pursuing Jesus?

I must think ahead and pre-decide: I will be devoted to Jesus.

Because of who God is and what he has done for me, I am willing to do anything and give up everything for him. God is first.

When you understand who God is, nothing else makes sense but to put him first.

These are the signs of being devoted:
- Where your mind goes
- Where your money goes
- How you make decisions
- How you spend your time
- What breaks your heart

I am going to seek God first.

The devil doesn't need to destroy you if he can distract you.
His plan is to detour you from your devotion by distracting
you from coming to Jesus, so you don't have the
connection that can empower your decisions.

Your enemy wants to pull you apart, divide your mind, discourage
your faith, and distract you from what matters most.

To prioritize our devotion to Jesus, we have to minimize our distractions.

My life is too valuable, my calling too great, and my God too good
to waste my time distracted by things that do not matter.

You'll have to say no to some good things to say yes to what's best.

A rule of life is a set of intentional rhythms
that help us to do the following:
- stay connected to Jesus;
- know him more;
- become more and more like him;
- create spiritual, relational, or vocational practices;
- align our priorities, values, and passions with the way
  we live our lives;
- overcome distractions, to not be so scattered and
  hurried and reactive and exhausted;
- start living for an audience of one.

To spend undistracted time with Jesus, pre-decide and prioritize
an intentional strategy that will include these three things:
- a time
- a place
- a plan

God is what matters, so I will be devoted to putting him first.
God is devoted to you. He put you first. Let's put him first.

PART 2 SCRIPTURES

They devoted themselves to the apostles' teaching and to
fellowship, to the breaking of bread and to prayer.

—Acts 2:42

No one can serve two masters. Either you will hate the one and
love the other, or you will be devoted to the one and despise the
other. You cannot serve both God and money.

—Matthew 6:24

But seek first his kingdom and his righteousness, and all these
things will be given to you as well.

—Matthew 6:33

Jesus replied: "Love the Lord your God with all your heart and
with all your soul and with all your mind."

—Matthew 22:37

Anyone who loves their father or mother more than me is not
worthy of me; anyone who loves their son or daughter more than
me is not worthy of me. Whoever does not take up their cross
and follow me is not worthy of me.

—Matthew 10:37–38

Set your minds on things above, not on earthly things.

—Colossians 3:2

For where your treasure is, there your heart will be also.

—Matthew 6:21

Do not conform to the pattern of this world, but be transformed
by the renewing of your mind. Then you will be able to test and
approve what God's will is—his good, pleasing and perfect will.

—Romans 12:2

So then, be careful how you walk, not as unwise people but as wise, making the most of your time, because the days are evil. Therefore do not be foolish, but understand what the will of the Lord is.

—Ephesians 5:15–17 NASB

Then the King will say to those on his right, "Come, you who are blessed by my Father; take your inheritance, the kingdom prepared for you since the creation of the world. For I was hungry and you gave me something to eat, I was thirsty and you gave me something to drink, I was a stranger and you invited me in, I needed clothes and you clothed me, I was sick and you looked after me, I was in prison and you came to visit me."

Then the righteous will answer him, "Lord, when did we see you hungry and feed you, or thirsty and give you something to drink? When did we see you a stranger and invite you in, or needing clothes and clothe you? When did we see you sick or in prison and go to visit you?"

The King will reply, "Truly I tell you, whatever you did for one of the least of these brothers and sisters of mine, you did for me."

—Matthew 25:34–40

Come to me, all you who are weary and burdened, and I will give you rest. Take my yoke upon you and learn from me, for I am gentle and humble in heart, and you will find rest for your souls.

—Matthew 11:28–29

All you thirsty ones, come to me! Come to me and drink! Believe in me so that rivers of living water will burst out from within you, from your innermost being, just like the Scripture says!

—John 7:37–38 TPT

I am the vine; you are the branches. If you remain in me and I in you, you will bear much fruit; apart from me you can do nothing.

—John 15:5

But the Holy Spirit produces this kind of fruit in our lives: love, joy, peace, patience, kindness, goodness, faithfulness, gentleness, and self-control.

—Galatians 5:22–23 NLT

She had a sister called Mary, who sat at the Lord's feet listening to what he said. But Martha was distracted by all the preparations that had to be made. . . . "Martha, Martha," the Lord answered, "you are worried and upset about many things, but few things are needed—or indeed only one. Mary has chosen what is better, and it will not be taken away from her."

—Luke 10:39–42

I am saying this for your benefit, not to place restrictions on you. I want you to do whatever will help you serve the Lord best, with as few distractions as possible.

—1 Corinthians 7:35 NLT

Set your gaze on the path before you.
With fixed purpose, looking straight ahead,
ignore life's distractions.

—Proverbs 4:25 TPT

Very early in the morning, while it was still dark, Jesus got up, left the house and went off to a solitary place, where he prayed.

—Mark 1:35

We love because he first loved us.

—1 John 4:19

Even before he made the world, God loved us and chose us in Christ to be holy and without fault in his eyes. God decided in advance to adopt us into his own family by bringing us to himself through Jesus Christ. This is what he wanted to do, and it gave him great pleasure.

—Ephesians 1:4–5 NLT

PART 3 TAKEAWAYS

I will be faithful.
We pre-decide to be faithful because we will never be faithful by accident.

Faithfulness honors God. And God honors faithfulness.

Because we are prone to pride, we are pre-deciding not to trust
ourselves but to trust God and live in faithfulness to him.

We are going to make three faithful pre-decisions:
1. Every interaction is an opportunity to add value.
2. Every resource is an opportunity to multiply.
3. Every prompting is an opportunity to obey God.

We don't have to live a natural, self-centered life. Because the
Holy Spirit lives inside of us, we can live a supernatural, others-
focused life. We can follow Jesus in living beyond the norm.

Jesus viewed every opportunity as a way to encourage, to meet needs,
to share God's grace. As his followers, we make up our minds to do
the same. We view every interaction as an opportunity to add value.
- We show grace.
- We meet needs.
- We forgive.
- We build up.
- We bless, serve, and speak words of life.

Multiplying what you've been given in the kingdom of God is faithfulness.

You are being faithful when you multiply the resources God has given you.

Because God is relational, he loves to speak to us in different ways:
- through his Word
- through circumstances
- through people
- through his Spirit

When God prompts, directs, or speaks to you,
your response will take faith.

If you commit to following Jesus, he will lead you. He will
prompt you, and faithfulness means feeling compelled to
obey even when you don't know what will happen next.

You have no idea what God might do when
you faithfully follow a prompting.

Obedience is our responsibility, the outcome is God's.

Pre-decide that you will be faithful in obeying God's every prompting.

Faith requires risk.

We want to live risk-free, but God wants us to live free to risk.

Your willingness to risk is based on the potential return.

When we stare at the risk, we're stopped by fear. But we can stare down the risk if we stay focused on the potential return.

You will overestimate what you can do in the short run but vastly underestimate what God can do through a lifetime of faithfulness.

When you're faithful with a little, God will trust you with much.

PART 3 SCRIPTURES

His master replied, "Well done, good and faithful servant! You have been faithful with a few things; I will put you in charge of many things. Come and share your master's happiness!"

—**Matthew 25:21**

Look at the proud!
They trust in themselves, and their lives are crooked.
But the righteous will live by their faithfulness to God.

—**Habakkuk 2:4 NLT**

Do not let any unwholesome talk come out of your mouths, but only what is helpful for building others up according to their needs, that it may benefit those who listen.

—**Ephesians 4:29**

So do not worry, saying, "What shall we eat?" or "What shall we drink?" or "What shall we wear?" For the pagans run after all these things, and your heavenly Father knows that you need them. But seek first his kingdom and his righteousness, and all these things will be given to you as well. Therefore do not worry about tomorrow, for tomorrow will worry about itself. Each day has enough trouble of its own.

—Matthew 6:31–34

"Woman, where are they? Has no one condemned you?"

"No one, sir," she said.

"Then neither do I condemn you," Jesus declared. "Go now and leave your life of sin."

—John 8:10–11

Jesus said, "Feed my sheep."

—John 21:17

Do everything without complaining and arguing, so that no one can criticize you. Live clean, innocent lives as children of God, shining like bright lights in a world full of crooked and perverse people.

—Philippians 2:14–15 NLT

Holding out to them a Message of Life.

—Philippians 2:16 WNT

And now, compelled by the Spirit, I am going to Jerusalem, not knowing what will happen to me there.

—Acts 20:22

And without faith it is impossible to please God.

—Hebrews 11:6

Whoever can be trusted with very little can also be trusted with much.

—Luke 16:10

PART 4 TAKEAWAYS

I will be an influencer.

Jesus said, "Go into the world and shine," not
"go into your homes and hide."

To be salt and light, we're going to pre-decide to influence with our

1. prayers,
2. example, and
3. words.

Prayer must be a strategic part of our influence.

- Be watchful for open doors to proclaim Christ.
- Be wise in the way you act toward those who are outside the faith.
- Make the most of every opportunity to share Jesus, always ready to give graceful answers to everyone.

Talk to God about people who are far from him.

- Pray that God will give you open doors to share Christ with people who are far from him.
- Pray that others who are close to God will share Christ with people who are far from him.
- Pray that people who are far from God will receive the message of Christ and walk through those open doors.

When we pray for open doors, God will open some.

We've been called to go. To be salt and light. To season. To shine. To share Jesus.

If you want to effect change in people's lives by pointing them to Jesus, start by praying for them.

Pre-decide to pray for people who are far from God:

- Pray that God would open their hearts.
- Pray that God would give them spiritual sight to understand and accept the gospel.
- Pray that God would lead them to repentance.
- Pray that God would give you the words to say to them.

I will influence with my example.

When you know who you are, you know what to do.

As salt, you preserve, heal, and create thirst for God in others.

As light, you don't run from the darkness, you shine in it.

God will show up and show off.

When we live as salt and light, people will notice and be changed.

Like Jesus with the woman at the well, start with the superficial, then move to the spiritual and then the personal in the most respectful, gracious way possible.

You are an influencer, and God wants to use you.

Knowing how patient and persistent God has been with us, we need to show that same patience and persistence to the people God loves. We need to commit to the long game.

PART 4 SCRIPTURES

You are the salt of the earth. But if the salt loses its saltiness, how can it be made salty again? It is no longer good for anything, except to be thrown out and trampled underfoot.

You are the light of the world. A town built on a hill cannot be hidden. Neither do people light a lamp and put it under a bowl. Instead they put it on its stand, and it gives light to everyone in the house. In the same way, let your light shine before others, that they may see your good deeds and glorify your Father in heaven.

—Matthew 5:13–16

And then he told them, "Go into all the world and preach the Good News to everyone."

—Mark 16:15 NLT

When the teachers of the law who were Pharisees saw him eating with the sinners and tax collectors, they asked his disciples: "Why does he eat with tax collectors and sinners?"

On hearing this, Jesus said to them, "It is not the healthy who need a doctor, but the sick. I have not come to call the righteous, but sinners."

—Mark 2:16–17

Devote yourselves to prayer, being watchful and thankful. And
pray for us, too, that God may open a door for our message,
so that we may proclaim the mystery of Christ, for which I
am in chains. Pray that I may proclaim it clearly, as I should.
Be wise in the way you act toward outsiders; make the most
of every opportunity. Let your conversation be always full of
grace, seasoned with salt, so that you may know how to answer
everyone.

—**Colossians 4:2–6**

I always thank my God as I remember you in my prayers,
because I hear about your faith in the Lord Jesus and your love
for all the saints. I pray that you may be active in sharing your
faith, so that you will have a full understanding of every good
thing we have in Christ.

—**Philemon vv. 4–6 NIV 1984**

Pray also for me, that whenever I speak, words may be given me
so that I will fearlessly make known the mystery of the gospel,
for which I am an ambassador in chains. Pray that I may declare
it fearlessly, as I should.

—**Ephesians 6:19–20**

The Lord opened her heart to pay attention to what was said by
Paul.

—**Acts 16:14 ESV**

To open their eyes, so they may turn from darkness to light and
from the power of Satan to God.

—**Acts 26:18 NLT**

God may perhaps grant them repentance leading to a knowledge
of the truth, and they may come to their senses and escape from
the snare of the devil.

—**2 Timothy 2:25–26 ESV**

"Which of these three do you think was a neighbor to the man
who fell into the hands of robbers?" The expert in the law
replied, "The one who had mercy on him." Jesus told him, "Go
and do likewise."

—**Luke 10:36–37**

The crowd joined in the attack against Paul and Silas, and the magistrates ordered them to be stripped and beaten with rods. After they had been severely flogged, they were thrown into prison, and the jailer was commanded to guard them carefully. When he received these orders, he put them in the inner cell and fastened their feet in the stocks.

About midnight Paul and Silas were praying and singing hymns to God, and the other prisoners were listening to them. Suddenly there was such a violent earthquake that the foundations of the prison were shaken. At once all the prison doors flew open, and everyone's chains came loose. The jailer woke up, and when he saw the prison doors open, he drew his sword and was about to kill himself because he thought the prisoners had escaped. But Paul shouted, "Don't harm yourself! We are all here!"

The jailer called for lights, rushed in and fell trembling before Paul and Silas. He then brought them out and asked, "Sirs, what must I do to be saved?"

They replied, "Believe in the Lord Jesus, and you will be saved—you and your household." Then they spoke the word of the Lord to him and to all the others in his house.

—Acts 16:22–32

When Jesus spoke again to the people, he said, "I am the light of the world. Whoever follows me will never walk in darkness, but will have the light of life."

—John 8:12

The Spirit of the Lord is on me, because he has anointed me to proclaim good news to the poor.

—Luke 4:18

Now he had to go through Samaria. So he came to a town in Samaria called Sychar, near the plot of ground Jacob had given to his son Joseph. Jacob's well was there, and Jesus, tired as he was from the journey, sat down by the well. It was about noon.

When a Samaritan woman came to draw water, Jesus said to her, "Will you give me a drink?" (His disciples had gone into the town to buy food.)

The Samaritan woman said to him, "You are a Jew and I am a Samaritan woman. How can you ask me for a drink?" (For Jews do not associate with Samaritans.)

Jesus answered her, "If you knew the gift of God and who it is that asks you for a drink, you would have asked him and he would have given you living water."

"Sir," the woman said, "you have nothing to draw with and the well is deep. Where can you get this living water? Are you greater than our father Jacob, who gave us the well and drank from it himself, as did also his sons and his livestock?"

Jesus answered, "Everyone who drinks this water will be thirsty again, but whoever drinks the water I give them will never thirst. Indeed, the water I give them will become in them a spring of water welling up to eternal life."

The woman said to him, "Sir, give me this water so that I won't get thirsty and have to keep coming here to draw water."

He told her, "Go, call your husband and come back."

"I have no husband," she replied.

Jesus said to her, "You are right when you say you have no husband. The fact is, you have had five husbands, and the man you now have is not your husband. What you have just said is quite true."

"Sir," the woman said, "I can see that you are a prophet. Our ancestors worshiped on this mountain, but you Jews claim that the place where we must worship is in Jerusalem."

"Woman," Jesus replied, "believe me, a time is coming when you will worship the Father neither on this mountain nor in Jerusalem. You Samaritans worship what you do not know; we worship what we do know, for salvation is from the Jews. Yet a time is coming and has now come when the true worshipers will worship the Father in the Spirit and in truth, for they are the kind of worshipers the Father seeks. God is spirit, and his worshipers must worship in the Spirit and in truth."

The woman said, "I know that Messiah" (called Christ) "is coming. When he comes, he will explain everything to us."

Then Jesus declared, "I, the one speaking to you—I am he."

Just then his disciples returned and were surprised to find him talking with a woman. But no one asked, "What do you want?" or "Why are you talking with her?"

Then, leaving her water jar, the woman went back to the town and said to the people, "Come, see a man who told me everything I ever did. Could this be the Messiah?" They came out of the town and made their way toward him.

—John 4:4–30

PART 5 TAKEAWAYS

I will be generous.

We are all selfish, but no one thinks they're selfish.

We're conditioned to believe that our lives will be
incomplete until we acquire and accumulate more.
Our culture tells us it is more blessed to get.
Jesus offers a countercultural message. He says, "It is
more blessed to give than to receive" (Acts 20:35).

You will be blessed more when you give.

Living a life marked by intentional generosity is
meaningful beyond monetary measure. You sense God's
joy when he uses you to show his love to others.

No one accidentally becomes generous.

We want to
- sow generously so we can reap generously,
- see God's grace abound to us,
- be made rich in every way, and
- be so generous people thank God for us.

Generosity is not about what you have or don't
have. Generosity is about your heart.

If you're not generous now, you won't be generous later.

More money doesn't change who you are, it just reveals who you are.

If you want to be generous when you have more,
learn to be generous when you have less.

Because my identity is rooted in Jesus, I will be generous.
Giving is not just what I do. Generous is who I am.

Generous people plan to be generous.

Generous people plan out their generosity and stand firm.

Generous people ask God:
- "How can I give more?"
- "Where can I make a bigger difference?"
- "Who can I bless?"
- "How do I maximize what you have given me?"

Generosity is not spontaneous or haphazard, or driven by emotion. Generosity is intentional and strategic, and driven by a desire to honor God and live the kind of life he blesses.

Generous people have a plan.

An unhealthy financial cycle looks like this:

A healthy financial cycle looks like this:

We give God our first and best.
We trust God to bless the rest.

Generosity allows faith to replace fear.
Generosity allows blessing to replace worry.
Putting God first with your finances breaks the cycle.
God promises he will provide for us if we put him first.
Generous people round up.

We will not just raise our standard of living.
We will raise our standard of giving.

I was putting my trust in money and not in God.
I was trusting what I could see instead of trusting what God had said.

You cannot outgive God.

We are going to live like no one else, so we can give like no one else.

Generous is not just what we do, it's who we are.

Knowing that generosity never happens by accident,
we plan and stand firm in our generosity.

PART 5 SCRIPTURES

But generous people plan to do what is generous,
and they stand firm in their generosity.

—Isaiah 32:8 NLT

The heart is deceitful above all things
and beyond cure.

—Jeremiah 17:9

Remembering the words the Lord Jesus himself said: "It is more blessed to give than to receive.'"

—Acts 20:35

Remember this: Whoever sows sparingly will also reap sparingly, and whoever sows generously will also reap generously. Each man should give what he has decided in his heart to give, not reluctantly or under compulsion, for God loves a cheerful giver. And God is able to make all grace abound to you, so that in all things at all times, having all that you need, you will abound in every good work. . . . You will be made rich in every way so that you can be generous on every occasion, and through us your generosity will result in thanksgiving to God.

—2 Corinthians 9:6–8, 11 NIV 1984

Then he told them a story: "A rich man had a fertile farm that produced fine crops. He said to himself, 'What should I do? I don't have room for all my crops.' Then he said, 'I know! I'll tear down my barns and build bigger ones. Then I'll have room enough to store all my wheat and other goods. And I'll sit back and say to myself, "My friend, you have enough stored away for years to come. Now take it easy! Eat, drink, and be merry!"'"

—Luke 12:16–19 NLT

Do not store up for yourselves treasures on earth, where moths and vermin destroy, and where thieves break in and steal. But store up for yourselves treasures in heaven, where moths and vermin do not destroy, and where thieves do not break in and steal. For where your treasure is, there your heart will be also.

—Matthew 6:19–21

But seek first the kingdom of God and his righteousness, and all these things will be provided for you.

—Matthew 6:33 CSB

"Bring the whole tithe into the storehouse, that there may be food in my house. Test me in this," says the LORD Almighty, "and see if I will not throw open the floodgates of heaven and pour out so much blessing that there will not be room enough to store it."

—Malachi 3:10

You should tithe, yes, but do not neglect the more important things.

—Matthew 23:23 NLT

Give, and it will be given to you. A good measure, pressed down, shaken together and running over, will be poured into your lap. For with the measure you use, it will be measured to you.

—Luke 6:38

Honor the LORD with your wealth,
    with the firstfruits of all your crops;
then your barns will be filled to overflowing,
    and your vats will brim over with new wine.

—Proverbs 3:9–10

The purpose of tithing is to teach you always to put God first in your lives.

—**Deuteronomy 14:23 TLB**

As the heavens are higher than the earth,
 so are my ways higher than your ways
 and my thoughts than your thoughts.

—**Isaiah 55:9**

All day long he craves and craves,
 but the righteous gives and does not hold back.

—**Proverbs 21:26 ESV**

And if anyone wants to sue you and take your shirt, hand over your coat as well. If anyone forces you to go one mile, go with them two miles.

—**Matthew 5:40–41**

The next day he took out two denarii and gave them to the innkeeper. "Look after him," he said, "and when I return, I will reimburse you for any extra expense you may have."

—**Luke 10:35**

But Zacchaeus stood up and said to the Lord, "Look, Lord! Here and now I give half of my possessions to the poor, and if I have cheated anybody out of anything, I will pay back four times the amount."

—**Luke 19:8**

Now I want you to know, dear brothers and sisters, what God in his kindness has done through the churches in Macedonia. They are being tested by many troubles, and they are very poor. But they are also filled with abundant joy, which has overflowed in rich generosity. For I can testify that they gave not only what they could afford, but far more. And they did it of their own free will. They begged us again and again for the privilege of sharing.

—**2 Corinthians 8:1–4 NLT**

No one can serve two masters. Either you will hate the one and love the other, or you will be devoted to the one and despise the other. You cannot serve both God and money.

—**Luke 16:13**

Therefore everyone who hears these words of mine and puts them into practice is like a wise man who built his house on the rock.

—Matthew 7:24

PART 6 TAKEAWAYS

I will be consistent.

Without consistency, we are vulnerable to temptations, harmful addictions, destructive behavior, and our enemy's spiritual attacks. Inconsistency interrupts the intimacy you should have *with* others and the influence you could have *on* others. If your life is not what you want, it's likely because you've been infected with inconsistency.

It's time to make decisions change into commitment and then learn how to live out that commitment. And when you do, your consistency will change everything.

People with good intentions make promises, but people with consistency make progress.

Successful people do consistently what other people do occasionally. Process precedes progress.

Successful people do over and over what other people do every now and then. Consistent action creates consistent results.

It's not what we do occasionally that makes a difference. It's what we do consistently that matters.

If we are going to stick to our decisions, honor God, become everything we're meant to become, and live the life he has for us, we have to grow in our consistency.

A weak *what* is a problem.
A weak *why* is a deal killer.

You might have a *what*, but not a clear *why*.

If you aren't clear on your what, you'll never accomplish it.
You cannot do what you do not define.
If your why isn't strong enough, you won't accomplish
your what. Because your why drives your what.
We need to start with why.

If you want to grow in consistency, start with why.

We're pre-deciding to shift from willpower to why-power.

A strong why will make all the difference. You will find that
your why trumps excuses and defeats detractors.

When you know your why, you will find a way.

If you want to become more consistent, define your why. Go deep.
Pray. Look within. Tap into your passion. Start with why.

If you want to succeed, plan to fail.

Perfectionism is a roadblock to great decision-making.

Too often we're held back by an all-or-nothing mindset.

One day is an exception. Two or three is a pattern.
If you miss a day, don't miss two.

The illusion of perfection can keep us from getting started.
We're never going to be perfect, but we can be consistent.

Trying to be perfect doesn't work for anyone.
But consistency works for everyone.

Focusing on results is the downfall of people who want to be consistent.

If you fall in love with the process, you can win every day.

You are successful when you do what you need to do today.

Consistency isn't an event. It's a process.

Consistency creates momentum.

You can't be consistent on your own. But you are not on your own.

When you feel like quitting, remember why you started.

Form your team. Assemble your tribe. Gather your troops.
You can't, but with a couple of friends cheering you on and holding you accountable, you can. Two are better than one. Three? Even better.

I can't. God can.
With God's help, I will be consistent.

How will you be consistent?
1. Start with your why.
2. Plan to fail.
3. Fall in love with the process.
4. Assemble your team.

Whatever it is, you can do it, with God's help.

PART 6 SCRIPTURES

Therefore, my dear brothers and sisters, stand firm. Let nothing move you. Always give yourselves fully to the work of the Lord, because you know that your labor in the Lord is not in vain.

—1 Corinthians 15:58

A person without self-control
is like a city with broken-down walls.

—Proverbs 25:28 NLT

I don't really understand myself, for I want to do what is right, but I don't do it. Instead, I do what I hate. . . . I want to do what is right, but I can't. I want to do what is good, but I don't. I don't want to do what is wrong, but I do it anyway.

—Romans 7:15, 18–19 NLT

Daniel soon proved himself more capable than all the other administrators and high officers. Because of Daniel's great ability, the king made plans to place him over the entire empire. Then the other administrators and high officers began searching for some fault in the way Daniel was handling government affairs, but they couldn't find anything to criticize or condemn. He was faithful, always responsible, and completely trustworthy.

—Daniel 6:3–4 NLT

But when Daniel learned that the law had been signed, he went home and knelt down as usual in his upstairs room, with its windows open toward Jerusalem. He prayed three times a day, just as he had always done, giving thanks to his God.

—Daniel 6:10 NLT

The king was overjoyed and gave orders to lift Daniel out of the den. And when Daniel was lifted from the den, no wound was found on him, because he had trusted in his God.

—Daniel 6:23

Do you not know that your bodies are temples of the Holy Spirit, who is in you, whom you have received from God? You are not your own.

—1 Corinthians 6:19

So then, since we have a great High Priest who has entered heaven, Jesus the Son of God, let us hold firmly to what we believe. This High Priest of ours understands our weaknesses, for he faced all of the same testings we do, yet he did not sin. So let us come boldly to the throne of our gracious God. There we will receive his mercy, and we will find grace to help us when we need it most.

—Hebrews 4:14–16 NLT

Jesus Christ is the same yesterday and today and forever.

—Hebrews 13:8

I brought glory to you here on earth by completing the work you gave me to do. Now, Father, bring me into the glory we shared before the world began.

—John 17:4–5 NLT

Two people are better off than one, for they can help each other succeed. If one person falls, the other can reach out and help. But someone who falls alone is in real trouble. Likewise, two people lying close together can keep each other warm. But how can one be warm alone? A person standing alone can be attacked and defeated, but two can stand back-to-back and conquer. Three are even better, for a triple-braided cord is not easily broken.

—Ecclesiastes 4:9–12 NLT

Oh, what a miserable person I am! Who will free me from this life that is dominated by sin and death? Thank God! The answer is in Jesus Christ our Lord.

—Romans 7:24–25 NLT

I pray that the eyes of your heart may be enlightened in order that you may know the hope to which he has called you, the riches of his glorious inheritance in his holy people, and his incomparably great power for us who believe. That power is the same as the mighty strength he exerted when he raised Christ from the dead and seated him at his right hand in the heavenly realms.

—Ephesians 1:18–20

PART 7 TAKEAWAYS

I will be a finisher.

If you're not dead, you're not done. God has more for you.

Every decision you make is a vote on your future.

Every time you are strong in the Lord and persevere,
you cast a vote that you will be a finisher.

Pre-decide: When I commit, I do not quit.

You may see me struggle, but I promise you won't see me quit.

Perseverance is the path to greatness.

"Enthusiasm is common. Endurance is rare" (Angela Duckworth).

Successful people succeed because of grit, which means
- it's okay if you're not the most talented,
- it's not a problem if you don't know the right people,
- it's not the end of the world if you're not especially educated.

You can overcome, achieve your goals, and live an amazing, God-honoring life if you just keep putting one foot in front of the other.

We will be tempted to quit because we can't see the future.

When we grow weary, we remember who we're running for and we take the next step. You don't have to finish the race today. You just need to take one more step.

From the beginning, Jesus had pre-decided: *I am ready, devoted, faithful, influential, generous, and consistent, and when I commit, I don't quit, because I am a finisher.*

He fixed his eyes on us. Now we fix our eyes on him.

We strengthen our hearts when we fix our eyes on Jesus.

When we fix our eyes on Jesus, we put our confidence in God instead of ourselves.

When we fix our eyes on Jesus, we have confidence because we know we can do all things through his strength, and that our confidence will be rewarded.

PART 7 SCRIPTURES

Now finish the work, so that your eager willingness to do it may be matched by your completion of it, according to your means.
—2 Corinthians 8:11

It would be good for you to finish what you started.

—**2 Corinthians 8:10 NLT**

You then, my child, be strengthened by the grace that is in Christ Jesus.

—**2 Timothy 2:1 ESV**

But you should keep a clear mind in every situation. Don't be afraid of suffering for the Lord. Work at telling others the Good News, and fully carry out the ministry God has given you.

—**2 Timothy 4:5 NLT**

As for me, my life has already been poured out as an offering to God. The time of my death is near. I have fought the good fight, I have finished the race, and I have remained faithful. And now the prize awaits me—the crown of righteousness, which the Lord, the righteous Judge, will give me on the day of his return.

—**2 Timothy 4:6–8 NLT**

However, I consider my life worth nothing to me; my only aim is to finish the race and complete the task the Lord Jesus has given me—the task of testifying to the good news of God's grace.

—**Acts 20:24**

So let's not get tired of doing what is good. At just the right time we will reap a harvest of blessing if we don't give up.

—**Galatians 6:9 NLT**

> Let your eyes look straight ahead;
>   fix your gaze directly before you.
> Give careful thought to the paths for your feet
>   and be steadfast in all your ways.
> Do not turn to the right or the left.

—**Proverbs 4:25–27**

In this world you will have trouble. But take heart! I have overcome the world.

—**John 16:33**

Let us throw off everything that hinders and the sin that so easily entangles. And let us run with perseverance the race marked out for us, fixing our eyes on Jesus, the pioneer and perfecter of faith. For the joy set before him he endured the cross, scorning its shame, and sat down at the right hand of the throne of God.

—Hebrews 12:1–2

No, in all these things we are more than conquerors through him who loved us.

—Romans 8:37

Jesus said, "It is finished." With that, he bowed his head and gave up his spirit.

—John 19:30

Father, forgive them, for they do not know what they are doing.

—Luke 23:34

I have made you and I will carry you.

—Isaiah 46:4

Being confident of this, that he who began a good work in you will carry it on to completion until the day of Christ Jesus.

—Philippians 1:6

Consider him who endured such opposition from sinners, so that you will not grow weary and lose heart.

—Hebrews 12:3

Such confidence we have through Christ before God. Not that we are competent in ourselves to claim anything for ourselves, but our competence comes from God.

—2 Corinthians 3:4–5

So do not throw away your confidence; it will be richly rewarded. You need to persevere so that when you have done the will of God, you will receive what he has promised.

—Hebrews 10:35–36

CONCLUSION TAKEAWAYS

The power of pre-decision is what puts people on the path of success.

There are seven essential pre-decisions that will automatize many of the more important of those 35,000 decisions and will set us on a path to the abundant life Jesus offers.

God chose us. Now he's asking us if we'll choose him.

Let's pre-decide:
- I will be ready.
- I will be devoted.
- I will be faithful.
- I will be an influencer.
- I will be generous.
- I will be consistent.
- I will be a finisher.

CONCLUSION SCRIPTURES

Now listen! Today I am giving you a choice between life and death, between prosperity and disaster.

—Deuteronomy 30:15 NLT

Oh, that you would choose life, so that you and your descendants might live!

—Deuteronomy 30:19 NLT

For the LORD has chosen Jacob to be his own,
Israel to be his treasured possession.

—Psalm 135:4

He chose the tribe of Judah,
Mount Zion, which he loved.

—Psalm 78:68

I have chosen David to rule my people Israel.

—**1 Kings 8:16**

He has chosen my son Solomon to sit on the throne of the kingdom of the LORD over Israel.

—**1 Chronicles 28:5**

David said to Michal, "It was before the LORD, who chose me."

—**2 Samuel 6:21**

Choose this day whom you will serve, whether the gods your fathers served in the region beyond the River, or the gods of the Amorites in whose land you dwell. But as for me and my house, we will serve the LORD.

—**Joshua 24:15 ESV**

You can make this choice by loving the LORD your God, obeying him, and committing yourself firmly to him. This is the key to your life.

—**Deuteronomy 30:20 NLT**

If we are faithless, he remains faithful, for he cannot disown himself.

—**2 Timothy 2:13**

Jesus Christ is the same yesterday and today and forever.

—**Hebrews 13:8**

Even before he made the world, God loved us and chose us in Christ to be holy and without fault in his eyes. God decided in advance to adopt us into his own family by bringing us to himself through Jesus Christ. This is what he wanted to do, and it gave him great pleasure.

—**Ephesians 1:4–5 NLT**

Jesus said, "It is finished."

—**John 19:30**

Notes

1. Asha C. Gilbert, "Man Thought He Had Water Stuck in His Ear and Used a Blow Dryer. Turns Out It Was a Cockroach," *USA Today*, January 13, 2022, www.usatoday.com/story/news/world/2022/01/13/man-finds-roach-ear-new-zealand/6513642001/.
2. Heidi Zak, "Adults Make More Than 35,000 Decisions Per Day. Here Are Four Ways to Prevent Mental Burnout," Inc., January 21, 2020, www.inc.com/heidi-zak/adults-make-more-than-35000-decisions-per-day-here-are-4-ways-to-prevent-mental-burnout.html.
3. Grant A. Pignatiello, Richard J. Martin, and Ronald L. Hickman Jr., "Decision Fatigue: A Conceptual Analysis," *Journal of Health Psychology* 25, no. 1 (January 2020): 123–35, www.ncbi.nlm.nih.gov/pmc/articles/PMC6119549/.
4. Chip Heath and Dan Heath, *Decisive: How to Make Better Choices in Life and Work* (New York: Crown Business, 2013).
5. C. S. Lewis, *Mere Christianity* (San Francisco: HarperSanFrancisco, 2001), 132.
6. Ray Dalio, *Principles: Life and Work* (New York: Simon and Schuster, 2017), ix, 255.
7. P. M. Gollwitzer, C. Gawrilow, and G. Oettingen, "The Power of Planning: Self-Control by Effective Goal-Striving," *Self Control in Society, Mind, and Brain* (Oxford: Oxford Univ. Press, 2010), 279–96.
8. Jochen P. Ziegelmann, Aleksandra Luszczynska, Sonia Lippke, and Ralf Schwarzer, "Are Goal Intentions or Implementation Intentions Better Predictors of Health Behavior? A Longitudinal Study in Orthopedic Rehabilitation," *Rehabilitation Psychology* 52, no. 1 (2007), 97–102.
9. "Why Do We Overestimate Our Self-Control? The Restraint Bias, Explained," The Decision Lab, accessed June 8, 2023, www.thedecisionlab.com/biases/restraint-bias/.

10. But you don't have a chicken. And, by the way, you know you have a problem with overspending if, instead of laughing at that list, you thought, "Wait, what's a Guac-Lock? Maybe I need one of those!"

11. Kate Brombley, "All Is Discovered! Fly at Once!" *Study of Fandom* (blog), July 31, 2014, arthurcdoyle.wordpress.com/2014/07/31/all-is -discovered-fly-at-once/.

12. Michael Winnick, "Putting a Finger on Our Phone Obsession," People Nerds, accessed June 8, 2023, dscout.com/people-nerds/mobile -touches.

13. Sam Whiting, "Muni Driver Keeps an Eye Out for Her Passengers," *San Francisco Chronicle*, September 8, 2013, www.sfchronicle.com /entertainment/article/muni-driver-keeps-an-eye-out-for-her -passengers-4797691.php.

14. Yes, I'm still in counseling for the bobcat incident.

15. Ibid. (Ditto.)

16. Sadie Robertson Huff, "Are You an Influencer? Sadie Robertson Huff at Liberty University Convocation 2022," Sadie Robertson Huff, January 20, 2022, YouTube video, www.youtube.com/watch?v =FL8Jw6ZFCAM&feature=youtu.be.

17. Aaron Earls, "Christians Don't Share Faith with Unchurched Friends," Lifeway Research, September 9, 2021, research.lifeway.com/2021/09 /09/christians-dont-share-faith-with-unchurched-friends/.

18. Annabel Fenwick Elliot, "Window Seat or Aisle—What Does Your Choice Say about You?" *Telegraph*, March 18, 2019, www.telegraph.co .uk/travel/comment/window-versus-aisle-debate/.

19. Harriet Sherwood, "Religious Children Are Meaner Than Their Secular Counterparts, Study Finds," *Guardian*, November 6, 2015, www.theguardian.com/world/2015/nov/06/religious-children-less -altruistic-secular-kids-study.

20. Samantha Vincenty, "How to Deal with Selfish Friends, Family, and Partners," Oprah Daily, October 14, 2019, www.oprahdaily.com/life /relationships-love/a29416336/dealing-selfish-people/.

21. Sarah Cox, "Muscular Men Less Likely to Support Social and Economic Equality, Study Suggests," Brunel University London, May 22, 2017, www.brunel.ac.uk/news-and-events/news/articles/Muscular-men -less-likely-to-support-social-and-economic-equality-study-suggests.

22. Helen Fields, "Mulling Over a Decision Makes People More Selfish, Study Suggests," *Science*, September 19, 2012, www.science.org/content

/article/mulling-over-decision-makes-people-more-selfish-study
-suggests.

23. Shankar Vedantam, "Does Studying Economics Make You Selfish?"
NPR, February 21, 2017, www.npr.org/2017/02/21/516375434/does
-studying-economics-make-you-selfish.

24. Brad Tuttle, "Study: The Rich Really Are More Selfish," *Time*,
August 12, 2011, business.time.com/2011/08/12/study-the-rich-really
-are-more-selfish/.

25. Alexander Soutschek et al., "The Dopaminergic Reward System
Underpins Gender Differences in Social Preferences," *Nature Human
Behaviour* 1 (2017): 819–27, doi.org/10.1038/s41562-017-0226-y.

26. "Women Are More Selfish Than Men and More Likely to Bad-Mouth
Their Friends Says Study," *Daily Mail*, June 5, 2011, www.dailymail
.co.uk/news/article-1394507/Women-selfish-men-likely-bad-mouth
-friends-says-study.html.

27. Ryan W. Carlson et al., "Motivated Misremembering of Selfish
Decisions," *Nature Communications* 11 (2020), www.nature.com
/articles/s41467-020-15602-4.

28. These studies are cited in Arthur Brooks, "Why Giving Makes You
Happy," *New York Sun*, December 28, 2007, www.nysun.com/article
/opinion-why-giving-makes-you-happy.

29. Bill Fay, "Demographics of Debt," Debt.org, July 21, 2023, www.debt.org
/faqs/americans-in-debt/demographics/.

30. Who, I just learned, has a full name: Captain Horatio Magellan Crunch.
Who knew?

31. Dave Ramsey, "Live Like No One Else—Dave Ramsey's Story," The
Ramsey Show Highlights, August 15, 2014, YouTube video, www
.youtube.com/watch?v=r1NJzEYARlM.

32. "The Eight Benefits of Praying with Your Spouse," iMom, accessed
June 8, 2023, www.imom.com/8-benefits-praying-spouse/.

33. Zig Ziglar, "How to Think Correctly," Let's Become Successful, May 31,
2020, YouTube video, www.youtube.com/watch?v=QeOJ997dYxc.

34. Roger Kahn, *The Boys of Summer* (New York: Harper Perennial, 2006),
224.

35. Jeff Haden, "A Study of 800 Million Activities Predicts Most New
Year's Resolutions Will Be Abandoned on January 19: How to Create
New Habits That Actually Stick," *Inc.*, January 3, 2020, www.inc.com
/jeff-haden/a-study-of-800-million-activities-predicts-most-new

-years-resolutions-will-be-abandoned-on-january-19-how-you
-cancreate-new-habits-that-actually-stick.html.

36. Yes, it's a real thing: Johnathan David, "Bearded Dragons as Emotional Support Pets," Council for Disability Awareness, August 6, 2020, blog .disabilitycanhappen.org/bearded-dragons-as-emotional-support-pets/.

37. Martin Seif and Sally Winston, "Behind Chronic Indecisiveness: Perfectionism," *Psychology Today*, November 25, 2021, www .psychologytoday.com/us/blog/living-sticky-mind/202111/behind -chronic-indecisiveness-perfectionism.

38. *The Office*, season 6, episode 11, "Shareholder Meeting," directed by Charles McDougall, written by Justin Spitzer, aired November 19, 2009, on NBC.

39. "Cognitive Distortions: All-or-Nothing Thinking," Cognitive Behavioral Therapy Los Angeles, accessed June 8, 2023, cogbtherapy .com/cbt-blog/cognitive-distortions-all-or-nothing-thinking.

40. Dominic Smithers, "Brazilian Jiu-Jitsu Trained Jogger Kills Cougar with Bare Hands after It Attacks Him," Sport Bible, February 5, 2019, www.sportbible.com/news/animals-runner-killed-cougar-with-his -bare-hands-after-it-attacked-him-20190205.

41. Natalie Burg, "To Be Successful, You Need More Than Just Goals— You Need Friends," *Forbes*, December 3, 2018, www.forbes.com/sites /colehaan/2018/12/03/to-be-successful-you-need-more-than-just -goals--you-need-friends/?sh=447338ae7454.

42. "The Importance of Having a Support System," Mental Health First Aid, August 6, 2020, www.mentalhealthfirstaid.org/2020/08/the -importance-of-having-a-support-system/.

43. "Manage Stress: Strengthen Your Support Network," American Psychological Association, last updated October 21, 2022, https://www.apa .org/topics/stress/manage-social-support#:~:text=Experts%20say%20 that%20almost%20all,esteem%20and%20sense%20of%20autonomy.

44. Dictionary.com, s.v. "synergy," accessed June 8, 2023, www.dictionary .com/browse/synergy.

45. Mission, "The Most Popular Productivity Pieces of Wisdom from David Allen," Medium, December 4, 2017, https://medium.com/the-mission /the-most-popular-productivity-pieces-of-wisdom-from-david-allen -72ffe70ac7b9.

46. Angela Duckworth, *Grit: The Power of Passion and Perseverance* (New York: Scribner, 2018), 58.

47. "U2: The Rock 'n Roll Money Trail," *Independent* (Ireland), March 6, 2009, www.independent.ie/entertainment/music/u2-the-rock-n-roll-money-trail-26519131.html.

48. Will Smith, "Will Smith Motivation," Young Urban Project, October 4, 2020, YouTube video, youtu.be/EUtaTkDJs-k.

49. IMDb, *Apollo 13* (1995), Gene Kranz (Ed Harris) quotations, www.imdb.com/title/tt0112384/characters/nm0000438.

50. "Florence Chadwick," *Wikipedia*, last edited May 18, 2023, https://en.wikipedia.org/wiki/Florence_Chadwick#Biography.

51. "About," Erik Weihenmayer (website), accessed June 8, 2023, erikweihenmayer.com/about-erik/.

52. Robert Krulwich, "Successful Children Who Lost a Parent—Why Are There So Many of Them?" NPR, October 16, 2013, www.npr.org/sections/krulwich/2013/10/15/234737083/successful-children-who-lost-a-parent-why-are-there-so-many-of-them.

53. Brent Bowers, "Study Shows Stronger Links between Entrepreneurs and Dyslexia," *New York Times*, November 5, 2007, www.nytimes.com/2007/12/05/business/worldbusiness/05iht-dyslexia.4.8602036.html.

54. Graham Winfrey, "Malcolm Gladwell on Why You Need Adversity to Succeed," Inc., November 12, 2014, www.inc.com/graham-winfrey/malcolm-gladwell-on-why-entrepreneurs-need-adversity-to-succeed.html.

55. "'Gentleman Jim' Corbett Knocks Out John L. Sullivan, 1892," Eyewitness to History, accessed June 8, 2023, www.eyewitnesstohistory.com/corbett.htm.

56. "Derek Redmond's Emotional Olympic Story," Olympics, October 31, 2011, YouTube video, youtu.be/t2G8KVzTwfw.

57. Goalcast, "Kobe Bryant—Advice on How to Leave Your Mark," Facebook, March 14, 2020, www.facebook.com/goalcast/videos/197096971705583/.

58. Goalcast, "Kobe Bryant."

59. Goalcast, "Kobe Bryant."

60. Scott Davis and Connor Perrett, "Kobe Bryant's Work Ethic Was Unmatched, Here Are Twenty-Four Examples," Insider, updated January 26, 2023, www.businessinsider.com/kobe-bryant-insane-work-ethic-2013-8.

61. Davis and Perrett, "Kobe Bryant's Work Ethic."

62. Davis and Perrett, "Kobe Bryant's Work Ethic."

63. Davis and Perrett, "Kobe Bryant's Work Ethic."

64. Goalcast, "Kobe Bryant."

65. *Theological Wordbook of the Old Testament*, eds. R. L. Harris, G. L. Archer Jr., and B. K. Waltke (Chicago: Moody Press, 1980), s.v. 231 בָּחַר, *bahar*.

66. *Theological Wordbook of the Old Testament*.

67. *Theological Wordbook of the Old Testament*.

68. Steven Skiena and Charles B. Ward, "Who's Biggest? The Hundred Most Significant Figures in History," *Time*, December 10, 2013, ideas .time.com/2013/12/10/whos-biggest-the-100-most-significant-figures -in-history/.

Winning the War in Your Mind

Change Your Thinking, Change Your Life

Craig Groeschel

More Than 500,000 Copies Sold!

Are your thoughts out of control—just like your life? Do you long to break free from the spiral of destructive thinking? Let God's truth become your battle plan to win the war in your mind!

We've all tried to think our way out of bad habits and unhealthy thought patterns, only to find ourselves stuck with an out-of-control mind and an off-track daily life. Pastor and *New York Times* bestselling author Craig Groeschel understands deeply this daily battle against self-doubt and negative thinking, and in this powerful book he reveals the strategies he has discovered to change your mind and your life for the long-term.

Drawing on Scripture and the latest findings of brain science, Groeschel lays out practical strategies that will free you from the grip of harmful, destructive thinking and enable you to live the life of joy and peace that God intends you to live. *Winning the War in Your Mind* will help you:

- Learn how your brain works and see how to rewire it.
- Identify the lies your enemy wants you to believe.
- Recognize and short-circuit your mental triggers for destructive thinking.
- See how prayer and praise will transform your mind.
- Develop practices that allow God's thoughts to become your thoughts.

God has something better for your life than your old ways of thinking. It's time to change your mind so God can change your life.

Winning the War in Your Mind for Teens also available!

Available in stores and online!

The Power to Change

Mastering the Habits That Matter Most

Craig Groeschel

Life-Changing Spiritual and Practical Strategies for True Transformation.

Nothing is more frustrating than knowing you need to change and trying to change, but failing to change. You feel stuck, no matter how hard you try. Craig Groeschel, bestselling author of *Winning the War in Your Mind*, knows what it's like to be caught in that cycle. That was his own story—until he discovered these practical and biblical principles for experiencing lasting change.

In *The Power to Change*, Groeschel will help you find true change in your relationships, habits, and thoughts by unpacking:

- How God's power, not your willpower, leads to true transformation
- The real reasons you do what you do
- Why falling isn't failure
- The power of creating small habits that lead to big change
- How to choose what you want most over what you want now

A powerful blend of biblical wisdom and fascinating psychology, *The Power to Change* includes helpful exercises, real-life stories, and life-changing spiritual insights. Whether you are trying to lose weight, breathe new life into your marriage, read the Bible more, get out of debt, or give up an addiction, Craig's step-by-step, time-tested strategies will equip you to start living the life God wants for you.

Available in stores and online!

Lead Like It Matters

Seven Leadership Principles for a Church That Lasts

Craig Groeschel

Discover the secret to igniting a life-giving, soul-transforming, people-inspiring movement in your organization, church, or ministry—and the trick to keeping the momentum going.

In *Lead Like It Matters*, *New York Times* bestselling author and pastor Craig Groeschel shares the transformative insights he has learned about how to effectively build a thriving, enduring ministry and organization.

Using the leadership skills he has mastered as the founder and senior pastor of Life.Church—one of the largest churches in the world and an organization that Glassdoor has named a #1 US Best Place to Work—he combines straight talk and wry honesty with biblical and leadership principles to equip you to:

- Recognize when your organization or ministry has the indefinable but tangible "it" that leads to success
- Identify and implement seven leadership principles for a church that lasts
- Ignite a fire in your team to leave behind "what we've always done" for the meaningful ministry you know is possible
- Discover the three areas every leader must master for success

Praise for *Lead Like It Matters*:

> "My friend Craig Groeschel is the visionary and pioneer of America's largest church. In *Lead Like It Matters*, he's generous enough to share the most important lessons he has learned along the way. This isn't just an insightful and interesting book, it's a game-changing guide to leading with purpose."
>
> —Steven Furtick, lead pastor, Elevation Church; *New York Times* bestselling author, *Crash the Chatterbox*; *Greater*; and *(Un)Qualified*

Available in stores and online!

Dangerous Prayers
Because Following Jesus Was
Never Meant to Be Safe

Do you ever wonder, "Why doesn't God answer my prayers?" Pastor Craig Groeschel will show you how to pray the prayers that search your soul, break your bad habits, and send you to pursue the calling God has for you. Discover the power of authentically communicating with God, breaking out of the restrictive "spiritual safety bubble," and expanding your faith in what is possible with God, gaining the courage it takes to pray dangerous prayers.

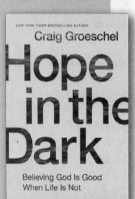

Hope in the Dark
Believing God Is Good When Life Is Not

In the midst of great pain, we may wonder whether God really cares about us. Pastor Craig Groeschel invites us to wrestle with our questions and doubts while honoring our faith and asking God to heal our unbelief. Rediscover faith in the character, power, and presence of God.

The Christian Atheist
Believing in God but Living
As If He Doesn't Exist

Join Pastor Craig Groeschel for a frank and raw conversation as he unpacks his personal walk toward an authentic, God-honoring life.

Liking Jesus
Intimacy and Contentment in a
Selfie-Centered World

Learn how breaking unmanageable digital depen-
dencies can bring a balance of spiritual depth and
human engagement back to your life.

Soul Detox
Clean Living in a Contaminated World

Examine the spiritual toxins poisoning your
relationship with God and learn about ways to remain focused on God's holy standards.

Fight
Winning the Battles That Matter Most

Uncover your true identity as a powerful man with
a warrior's heart and find the strength to fight
battles you know must be won.

Divine Direction
Seven Decisions That Will Change Your Life

Take your life to wonderful and unexpected places
only God could have planned by understanding
how the choices you make connect you to God.

Daily Power
365 Days of Fuel for Your Soul

Develop a consistent, daily pursuit of Jesus as
Pastor Craig Groeschel shares insights from his
life that you can apply to almost every area of your
own life.

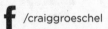 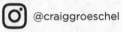

Personal. Practical. Powerful.

CRAIG GROESCHEL
LEADERSHIP PODCAST

Subscribe to the **Craig Groeschel Leadership Podcast** on Apple Podcasts or wherever you listen to podcasts.

Visit **www.life.church/leadershippodcast** to find the episode videos, leader guides, discussion questions, and more.

 Apple Podcasts

 Spotify

 Google Podcasts

 YouTube

From the Publisher

GREAT BOOKS

ARE EVEN BETTER WHEN THEY'RE SHARED!

Help other readers find this one

- Post a review at your favorite online bookseller

- Post a picture on a social media account and share why you enjoyed it

- Send a note to a friend who would also love it—or better yet, give them a copy

Thanks for reading!